EXPLORING WASHINGTON'S SMALLER CITIES

by Clifford Burke

QB

Design and illustration: Kris Ekstrand Molesworth

ISBN 0-93189-03-9

Quartzite Books
P. O. Box 1931
Mount Vernon, WA 98273

Manufactured in the United States of America

1 2 3 4 5 6 7 8 9 10

CONTENTS

ACKNOWLEDGEMENTS

Most of the help for this book came from anonymous voices on the ends of telephone lines and patient but unnamed workers at chambers of commerce, cab companies, city offices, bars, burger stands, etc. To all those people who daily provide the information, rest and sustenance to visitors to these smaller cities I and my fellow travelers are grateful. And all those who work tirelessly to make these places more interesting or more colorful, we all owe a debt for the fun we have when we visit.

In turning the visits into a book I had some special help from: David and Stephanie Slabaugh, Delphine Haley, Molly Cook of Skagit Bay Books in La Conner, Suzanne Butler, Charmaine Johannes, Carl Molesworth, Fenicia, Clea and Margaret Burke, Glenn Desjardin,Tom Davis, Raisin Hubbard, Jim Halm and Jack and Grace Hubbard.

I owe a special debt of gratitude to the mostly unsung authors of the Washington Writers Project of the Works Progress Administration, the WPA, whose guide to the state was first published in 1941. Some of the prose in that book is just beautiful, and the sensitive fondness for this region, especially for the cities, has been an ongoing source of inspiration.

And I want especially to thank my mother, Claire S. Baldwin, and dedicate this book to her. It is her love of our native Puget Sound country that I have inherited, and she has been indefatigable as a scout in those distant small cities.

Thanks, Mom.

Introduction: Looking at Smaller Cities

Going from place to place around Washington State you can't help but notice the great and varied beauty of the region. That's what makes the Pacific Northwest such a popular destination for tourists; that's what the brochures offer you and none of it is faked up. Plentiful are the rewards of moving around: the views, the sounds, the different water and winds and weather. And as you travel around the state you come repeatedly upon the recurrent small city, the crossroads of major highways and the places where land and water, commerce and culture meet.

While natural beauties are found in parks and wilderness, mountains, lakes and rivers and so on, in its cities a region describes itself. Cities are the focus of communication of all kinds, not just transport, and if you want to see what the people are like, they gather and express themselves in these urban centers.

Cities are the focus of history, too, and they accumulate it as they go. The juxtapositions of cultural artifacts piling up alongside one another make a place visually and actively interesting. Sometimes these juxtapositions are anything but attractive, and in all cities, even the pretty ones, there are places where gawdawful heaps, industrial and otherwise, crowd the eye of the most optimistic viewer.

But the rush to the suburbs and the waning period of the inner city is over. The rebirth of the urban core is visible in specific interesting ways, ways more clearly seen, perhaps, in these smaller places than in large cities where wholesale urban renewal chops up great chunks of a downtown at a time. In the smaller cities patterns are more apparent. Sometimes, too, it's easier to see possibilities, just as the hindrances are more obvious-- an antique restoration in an attractive spot; an industrial relic ruining the view. Sometimes it takes some selective looking to see how we could go about, to twist Joaquin Miller's phrase a little bit, rebuilding the City Beautiful.

THE APPROACH

For many travelers these smaller cities are merely necessary waystations, places to refuel, refect, sleep and move on, especially if the reason for travel is business or the goal the wilderness beyond. Often there is little time beyond the convention center, calls to make and late HBO at the motel. Much of the information about a place that's available to the visitor is really only pertinent to the people who live there.

This guide is intended to give the visitor on a short stay a way of looking at a town that makes its potential apparent, while providing access to sights and activities fitting a visit of a few hours or a few days. The approach, or "view" of each of the cities is organized in pretty much the same way, as shown in the table of contents. It should be possible to get quickly ito the heart of a city and use the time that's available pleasantly, in ways that correspond to personal interests. The only other really necessary tool is a local newspaper or a current schedule of community events, available from visitors centers.

APOLOGIES

The cities included here were chosen according to several criteria, many of them purely personal and arbitrary. The first concern was to cover the state in such a way that the great variety and beauty of its various parts might also be seen. I discovered early on that cities like Tacoma and Everett are too large to fit into the model I set for myself-- Spokane is really too large as well, but is such a wonderful place to visit that I couldn't resist. Others have written whole guidebooks to Spokane.

Of the smaller cities that are not included I can only plead lack of time, paucity of tourist interest, and prejudice-- I could not bring myself, for instance, to recommend to visitors the Nuclear City of Richland. Of those included I like some places better than others, but I hope my preferences aren't too obvious.

Finally, cities are not frozen in time like books. They are dynamic and constantly changing according to the economy, the government, or the weather. Sometimes restaurants, art galleries, boutiques seem to come and go with the seasons, and I had to stop somewhere. If you find a special place I missed, let me know.

HIGH HOPES

Perhaps my years living in rural Washington have made me inordinately fond of the urban environment, but I love the complex sights, sounds and interactions, the very pavements of cities large and small. And I see hope for people living in new ways in cities, ways that concentrate our cultural and economic and educational processes in a balanced environment, one that frees up the pressure on the fragile and beautiful land around us.

As you visit the cities of Washington I hope you'll see them in the context of their terrain, as repositories of our history and culture that it is worthwhile for us all to preserve, and as places with the potential for the highest ideals of people living and working together. And remember, when you visit these smaller cities: have some fun.

Port Angeles
by the Sea

Along the Strait of Juan de Fuca, on the north ledge of the Olympic Mountains, where the water and the weather sweep in from the Pacific Ocean and the water from all those rivers and mountains around Puget Sound flows back through the Strait and out to sea, a sandspit called Ediz Hook forms a protected natural harbor, inside of which grew up the city of Port Angeles.

Due south of the city, Hurricane Ridge in the Olympics rises directly, forming a rugged backdrop and providing a rich visual scene, with views taking in the blue water of the strait and snow-covered peaks at the same time.

Port Angeles is a real port city, on a scale that allows you to see the bones and sinew of ocean-going commerce. Here you can debark from a foreign port (Victoria, B.C.) on the downtown docks, from a vessel that looks almost as if it could have come from Singapore. Indeed, in the small harbor there is usually some freighter flying an exotic flag, waiting to load up logs at the port.

Port Angeles has been pretty much like this since the early days. Logging and the handling of timber, lumber and timber products has motivated the place. What are now streets once were flumes and skid roads for scooting logs down from the nearby mountainsides; at the corner of Lincoln and First you can see a photo story of the building and filling of the streets. Even now one highway on the west side of town is devoted to the run of logging trucks down to the pier. Fishing, too, has been a mainstay since eons before white people ever came here, and persists today in a persistent commercial fishery, with buyers on the docks downtown and trawlers, seiners and gillnetters plying back and forth across the bay, and in sport fishing that draws deepwater anglers throughout the year.

The town of Port Angeles got a boost in the early days from the settlement of the Puget Sound Cooperative Colony, which, in a protest against importation of low-wage Chinese labor, developed as a workers' community here. Another important influence on the character of Port Angeles was the presence of the Navy, especially in the decades following World War I when most of the Pacific Fleet used this harbor as a home port. It's this ongoing transience of loggers, fishers, sailors, truckers, that gives Port Angeles a kind of impermanent, rough-hewn quality. But this is also a place with a monthly poetry reading at the college, a full-fledged symphony orchestra, and an international port of call. The tourists and recreationists, the workers, the artists and artisans, all mix comfortably amid the ever-present wildness, the ravines that still run through town, the looming forests and the towering Hurricane Ridge.

ARRIVALS

The road into Port Angeles is the northernmost loop of Highway 101, the inner coastal highway threading the three West Coast states. Most commonly, your arrival by car will be from the east, and you can see how well traveled that route from Port Townsend and Puget Sound is by the number of services located along the eastern access into town, the kind of auto-related sprawl found at the edges of cities everywhere. You see virtually none of those businesses on the western outskirts. As with many other communities, you need to break away from the fast lanes to see the town. In Port Angeles a peculiarity of the one-way streets can easily lead you into a loop of roadside businesses that takes you right back out of town the way you came. To avoid this rather dreary introduction to Port Angeles, avoid turning left and up the hill as you come into town from the east. Especially avoid Race Street and Lincoln Street, main thoroughfares to the west side, and save them for later exploration. Instead, turn right wherever you can, and get as close to the water as possible; try to start your visit to Port Angeles anywhere below the bluff.

If you arrive by bus, at the **Greyhound Depot**, you travel the same route, only you are dropped off right near the edge of the below-bluff, water's-edge, older part of town, and are within easy walking distance of the motels and the sights. Schedules from Seattle run daily. The Greyhound line hooks up with two county transit systems, so there are connections with Port Townsend, with surrounding smaller towns, and with some parks. The main transfer point for **Clallam County Transit**, affectionately called "The Bus," is at the corner of First & Cherry, where printed schedules are available. These county lines running to and from outlying areas are part of the reason Port Angeles has such a busy look about it. Specific routes around the city will get you to most of the places mentioned on the rest of these pages.

There are scheduled airline services to Port Angeles, arriving at the **Fairchild International Airport**. For schedules to and from Seattle and other nearby cities call **San Juan Airlines**. Taxi service from the airport to any of the downtown motels, via **Blue Top Cab**, costs about $6. County Transit line number 24 serves the airport hourly.

And you can arrive by sea at Port Angeles. The international ferry **Coho** plies the water between Victoria and Port Angeles. A walk-on ferry trip to Victoria and back for a day or an overnight stay is one of my top choices for an excursion, among the many excellent side trips you'll find on the North Peninsula. I'm not a collector of ferry trips, but I love the quality of arriving in a place by ship, especially watching the skyline of a city change and grow as the approach to dock is made-- it's a very special way to see Victoria and Port Angeles both.

PLACES TO STAY

In looking for a place to stay in Port Angeles, the

chance for a view of the port and the Strait vies with an opportunity to see the mountains rising up so sharply to the south. I decided that since the weather on the mountains is fickle and often obscures them, and the activity on the harbor is always interesting whatever the weather, that I'd look for views of the harbor as first preference. The fanciest and the closest in and the closest to the water is the **Red Lion Bayshore Inn**. It has a pool, restaurant and lounge-- the works-- and is literally next door to many of the attractions downtown. Conventions use the Bayshore a lot, so the desirable view rooms might be hard to get, and the place might be overrun.

Places on the bluff overlooking town have splendid views of both the mountains and the water. Easy to find because of the rather overlarge sign is the **Hill Haus Motel**, with a choice of mountain or water views, although the water views are more expensive. There's nothing fancy about the **Flagstone Motel**, but there's an excellent view of Hurricane Ridge from the upper rooms in the middle section, and you can just get a glimpse of the Strait from the door. Inexpensive views, and it's across from the old Congregational church, the oldest in town, now restored and a real estate office.

Two excellent bed & breakfast places on the bluff above the harbor offer some views, and different decor styles for folks who like this type of overnight stay. The **Tudor Inn** is a restored English-style home filled with European antiques and much help with skiing, bicycle and other excursions. In an American Colonial home, **Glen Mar** offers a full breakfast (my kind of place) and two rooms that look out on the mountains and the harbor. As in other places, bed & breakfasts emerge with the seasons, so check the phone book for new listings, or the referral service, **Bed & Breakfast Port Angeles**.

For campers and RV and trailer travelers, the North Olympic Peninsula offers a wealth of campgrounds and overnight motoring sites with and without hook-ups. Within the city of Port Angeles, **Lincoln Park** has 38 campsites and trailer spaces (but no hookups) and is close to downtown. For trailers and RVs, **City Center Trailer Park** is down in one of the canyons along Peabody Creek, cool and quiet in the summertime, and it's only three blocks from the ferry dock. **Welcome Inn Trailer Park** has tent camping available as well as hookups, and will arrange tours to Victoria, salmon charters, and other outings to augment your stay.

EATING OUT

If you step off the ferry or get out of your car down by the City Pier, there are two or three places to eat nearby, that might be handy if you want a quick munch, and we'll come back to those. But if you have the time and inclination for a meal, walk up into the town and try **The Greenery**, partly because it's a pleasant place serving thoughtful and well-prepared dishes for breakfast, lunch and dinner; also because it's a good introduction to Port Angeles-- not exactly a restored building, but fitting in well with the restorations that have begun here.

For other lunch and dinner places that have something of the place about them, you have to travel a little bit. Just to the east of downtown **Birney's** is a traditional family-style place with friendly folks all around and a surprising dedication to seafood, worthy of your notice. In a different style, on the west side of town, down by the marina among the log trucks, is **Smitty's**, where you can hang out around the gorgeous antique bar and backbar, or have a choice of gourmet burgers or a wide array of seafood in the jovial cafe. And a place that's very popular with the locals, doing excellent work in the steak and seafood line, is **The Bushwacker**, where there's also entertainment in the lounge most nights.

If you want to stay within walking distance, a colorful cheerful decor and sensitive and authentic Mexican cooking can be found at **La Casita**, open for lunch and dinner. And one of the places mentioned as being quite close is the **Hickory Dock** which has a walkup window open in the summers, and offers a tasty array of barbeque as well as seafood items such as smoked salmon and blackened cod.

But if you want fine dining, you have to travel up the hill east of town to **C'est Ci Bon** for a wonderful view and new French cooking that has earned an excellent region-wide reputation.

Since log truck drivers rise earlier than anybody, the venerable cafes open very early around Port Angeles. You can get breakfast at 5:30 at **Haguewood's** in the Red Lion, and the **Jury's Inn** is open all night. If you want to wait a little (till 7 am) you can get espresso and do breakfast continental style, or have one of the unusual breakfast specials at the **First Street Haven**, in a nicely restored brick building dated 1912.

The place is loaded with treats. If the delis and cafes haven't satiated you, there's always **Steve's Bakery** which, if you walk Port Angeles much at all you've probably passed several times. I held out for twice, then ducked in. For espresso, desserts and pastries, the **Coffee House Gallery** offers you a chance to take a break and see something of what the region has to offer in the visual arts. Or you can walk along the water to **Pisces Seafood**, local fresh fish dealer, to see what's come out of the sea that day, and have a crab or shrimp cocktail. In the summer there's a hot dog wagon working the corner of First and Lincoln. Did I leave out anything?

SEEING THE SIGHTS

Well fed, you've probably already seen much of the downtown tour: the docks, some of the old buildings, and the bluff. The full downtown visit should begin at the **City Pier**. Here is an ideal urban park, but it is also such an excellent focus for a look at the city, that it would be a shame to miss. The award-winning design of this park allows a multiplicity of uses, and puts visitors and residents alike into close contact with the sea's edge. Here visiting boats can find temporary moorage, and the activities of shipping and ferry travel are seen from the docks themselves, not from a distant viewpoint. Start at the observation deck at the end of the pier for a look at both the city and the harbor, and, on good days, glimpses of the mountains rising up behind. A walk west along Railroad Ave takes you past the Coho Ferry Dock and along the water for a couple of blocks. When you come up to the Port Dock, where logs are loaded for export, turn south for a block, then west again on Front. This route shows you several of the older buildings downtown, including a restored carriage house that is now a wine shop and a turn-of -the-century hotel and tavern. Follow Front to Lincoln, go south again for a block, then retrace your direction west along First Street. The photo mural along the Lincoln Street side of that corner building shows how Port Angeles turned log flumes into paved streets. On this walk you weave through the downtown streets of Port Angeles, and eventually you reach the Conrad Dyar Memorial Circle a fountain with benches for resting and watching the bustle of this small metropolis. Have you been noticing the flags and banners? If you can read flag-talk, they spell out "welcome."

At this point you are at the foot of the Laurel Street Stairs, and you have a choice to make. Either you continue along First, which will connect with Boat Haven Drive and lead you, if your pins hold out, to the Boat Haven with its archetypical dockside cafe and all the activity of the working docks. Or you can climb the steps and take in the view of the town, the harbor and Ediz Hook from the bluff. If you walk west along the bluff on Second Street you will come to James City Park and the head of a switchback walkway leading back down to First. If you walk east along Second you come again to Lincoln, and if you walk south up the hill you will pass the public library, with the old Carnegie library still in evidence, a replica of the Liberty Bell, and arrive at the **Old Clallam County Courthouse**, now a museum.

Other sightseeing trips really require a car, The Bus, or bicycles. A trip out Ediz Hook is well worth the time, for the view of the town seen in its setting of steep bluffs, hills and the mountains rising so dramatically to the south. Along the way are marinas, the Coast Guard station and lighthouse, and the Puget Sound Pilots' station, which sends pilots out to vessels entering the Sound. For a day on Ediz Hook, Bus number 27 travels the route in the morning and again in the afternoon.

Many of the people traveling through Port Angeles are bound for Hurricane Ridge and the north section of Olympic National Park. The eighteen-mile drive to the ridge is one of continuously surprising views as the road curves around precipices. There are numerous turnouts where you can stop and gaze. At the end of the road are a snack bar and an interpretive center, plus numerous trailheads for hiking and downhill and crosscountry skiing. For a guided sightseeing tour to Hurricane Ridge, call **Gray Line Tours** for schedules.

PARKS

Several of the city's parks have already been mentioned. The large **Lincoln Park** is adjacent to the fairgrounds. Besides having camping facilities, it has enough woods for quiet walks, play areas for the kids, sports facilities, and an authentic Indian longhouse and pioneer cabins. **City Pier**, besides providing a splendid introduction to the town and its environs, also provides a demonstration of the local relation to the sea in the exhibits presented at the **Fiero Marine Laboratory** during summer months. You can poke along the strip of beach where traveling Indians once made their camps, or watch fishing boats unloading at the buyers pier out from the somewhat garish new shopping complex called The Landing. The juxtapositions here give you an idea of the appropriate use of urban marine frontage and excessive use.

On **Ediz Hook** it's difficult to walk the seaward side of the sandspit because it has been reinforced all along with rock, but you can get a sense of the weather and the water outside the bay, and partake of the spectacular views of the mountains rising up behind the seaport town.

Several of the smaller parks around Port Angeles have various recreational facilities and are mentioned in the section on sports.

HISTORY AND ART

The premier historic building in the city is the old Clallam County Courthouse, which now houses the **Clallam County Historical Museum**. Built in 1914, this solid and distinctive red building occupies a commanding position on lawns in front of the ultramodern, solar heated, new courthouse just up the hill. Seeing the museum allows you a glimpse at some of the grandeur of the old building, including the original courtroom. Other exhibits are taken from pioneer life, implements, toys and other artifacts. Among the several galleries of historical displays, the Chamberlain Gallery exhibits rotating shows of regional art works, changing every three months.

On the road up to Hurricane Ridge, the Olympic National Park Visitors' Center houses the **Pioneer Memorial Museum.** Shown there, in typical Park Service style, are the natural features of the park, displays of early logging impedimenta and an Indian whaling canoe, weapons and tools. On the grounds is a restored homesteader's cabin complete with furnishings.

There are many side trips to be taken around the Peninsula, but one that is definitely worthwhile is the trip to Neah Bay and the **Makah Museum**, a hard 75-mile drive to the west on the seacoast. The museum is based on archeological finds at nearby Ozette, an ancient fishing village inundated and preserved for centuries by a mudslide. The insights into the spirit, culture and economy of the Makahs illustrated in the quiet galleries of the museum are somehow humbling and uplifting at the same time.

Art galleries in Port Angeles include the **Harbor Gallery** on the lower level of Harbortowne Mall, showing art and art objects by Peninsula artists and craftspersons. **The Woodbox** is an antique and handmade furniture store that also exhibits the work of local artists. And, mentioned above, the **Coffee House Gallery** has monthly shows on its walls.

Recently dedicated, the **Port Angeles Fine Art Center**, high on the hill near the College and commanding a wonderful overlook of the city, promises an ambitious program of art related events, artists in residence and rotating shows.

SHOPPING

If you take this whirlwind shopping tour through Port Angeles you will see that there are many of the name stores you'd expect, a couple of new downtown shopping malls, and generally enough activity among the boutiques to keep your interest piqued. Here are just a few notables. At the end of the waterfront area you'll find **Pisces Seafood**, where the mainstay is fresh fish, but where you can find a fair selection of seafood specialty items that will travel and keep. Just up the street, in a model of historic preservation and restoration, is **Carriage House Wines**, with an excellent selection of Northwest vintages and some of the old equestrian atmosphere still in evidence.

Walking on up to Front Street you come upon

the **Odyssey Bookshop**, a general-interest new book shop with used books in the back, and excellent, well-arranged sections on the Northwest, Northwest Indian cultures and travel. Walk on up to First and head east, and you'll come upon **The Woodbox**, already mentioned for its art exhibits, where you can browse amongst antique furniture and wooden serendipities. Further north on First you'll come upon **Treehouse Toys**, a toy store stuffed full, to the delight of any kids you might be dragging along.

Malls, which have not (to their credit and the town's) all fled to the hinterlands, include Harbortowne, The Landing, and Armory Square. And while you're at this shopping spree, notice the architecture, location and possiblities of the Lamonts Department Store.

A NIGHT ON THE TOWN

They don't exactly have barkers in the streets, and off season things can look a little dull at night, but if you scout around you'll find adequate entertainment.

Port Angeles supports a symphony orchestra that has been in existence for 54 years and plays a season of six concerts at the **Port Angeles High School Auditorium**, as well as a pops concert and other special performances. For specific dates call or write the **Port Angeles Symphony Orchestra**. Watch also for perfromances of the **Port Angeles Light Opera Company** in the same auditorium.

In other performing arts, the **Port Angeles Community Players** present a lively season in repertory at their own Playhouse near the College. The **Peninsula College Little Theatre** hosts student productions throughout the year. Also at the college, the **Peninsula Film Society** presents regular screenings from the obscure to the truly great. The Little Theatre is also the hall where the monthly **Foothills Poetry Series** is held, featuring poets from the Peninsula and around the Sound.

If it's loud music and suds you're after, the **Salty Dawg** is one of the town's more colorful taverns. In a building rightout of the early days, it has great sandwiches and a variety of entertainment varying from reggae to country to old rock 'n' roll. As a hangout, the reputation of the **M & C Tavern** has spread to the very edges of Puget Sound country, the one place I was told not to miss when I said I was traveling to Port Angeles: funky decor, honky-tonk piano, honkytonk bar. And for one of those places where there's always something going on, try **Aggie's**, a big motel with a restaurant and lounge that has live music and dancing most nights.

INDOOR AND OUTDOOR SPORTS

Port Angeles and the surrounding region offer a wealth of outdoor recreational activities, from boating and fishing in the Strait to crosscountry skiing and hiking at Hurricane Ridge, and many who come here are intent upon sports in the outlying areas. Mention has been made of the **Grey Line Tours** bus service to Hurricane Ridge; if you are planning to get up into the mountains you should stop at the **National Park Information Center** for current conditions. For outfitting any season, **Sorensen Sports** has equipment and advice for almost every mountain sport.

There are a number of fishing charters, most operating year round, for salmon, bottom fish and halibut. Many of the boats are moored at the **Port**

Angeles Boat Haven, so you can get by and have a look at them. To arrange charters call **Blue Dolphin Charters** or **Doug's Charters**. Out on Ediz Hook is **Thunderbird Boathouse** for fishing boat rentals and charters.

If you are interested in spectator sports, **Civic Field** is the playing arena for most team sports in the area. Racing enthusiasts will want to head out to **Port Angeles Speedway** for stock car racing May through September.

Sports facilities around town are quite extensive. Indoor swimming is at the **William Shore Memorial Pool**. The **YMCA** has racquetball courts, a gym for basketball and volleyball, a weight room, sauna, and other games and activities. It can be used by the day by visitors. Tennis courts are to be found at **Lincoln Park** and **Shane Park**, with lighted courts available at **Erickson Playfield**. Golf for a modest fee is played at the **Peninsula Golf Club**, an 18-hole course.

Bicyclists can find equipment and supplies for touring, and rentals for just poking around, at **Pedal 'n' Pack**, as well as good advice on routes, tours and terrain.

BIG EVENTS

The biggest annual event in these parts is the **Port Angeles Salmon Derby** and the ten-day festival that surrounds it, at the end of August through Labor Day. While the salmon derby at the end is the highlight, with as many as 2,000 people fishing for cash and other prizes, the Derby Days Festival attracts a lot of folks with interests other than fishing. Some of the events include a grand parade to kick things off, a classic car show, a salmon bake (of course!) and the inevitable square dance. On weekends there are arts and crafts booths set up on the City Pier. Pretty festive doings, and the weather is usually just terrific.

Most of the big events take place during the summer. Independence Day is celebrated with fireworks out on the harbor. Later in July comes the **Arts in Action Street Fair**, when the whole downtown area takes part, with arts and crafts booths on several streets, artisans doing ongoing demonstrations of their techniques, and a variety of performances going on sporadically. Late July is also usually the time of the **Civic Light Opera Association** summer performance series, over two weekends.

And in mid-August comes the **Clallam County Fair**, four days of pure Americana, complete with carnival, rodeo, and well-bred animals and birds and string beans and pies.

For specific dates of summer events call or write the Chamber of Commerce **Visitor Center** (*). Or just show up-- with all the comings and goings, ferries docking and departing, buses to and from the outback, folks heading into the mountains or out on the water, the place is always pretty festive in the summertime.

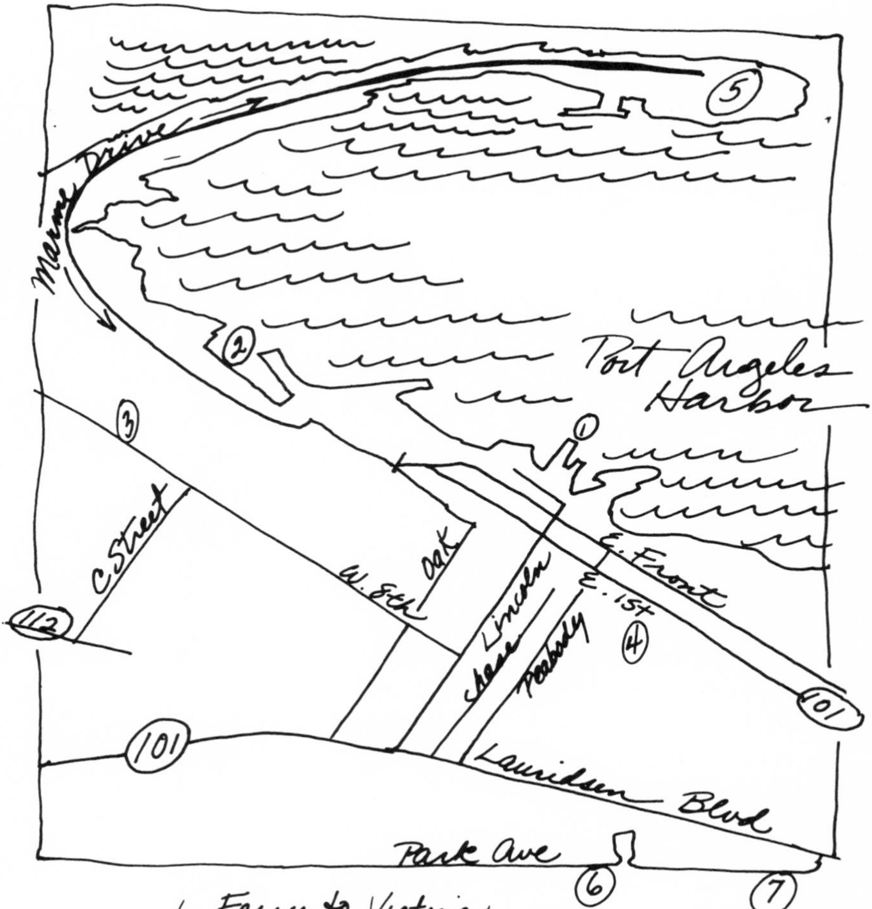

1. Ferry to Victoria
2. Marina
3. Shane Park
4. Webster Park
5. Ediz Hook
6. Pioneer Museum
7. Peninsula College

Downtown Port Angeles

Port Angeles Index

EDIZ HOOK..............................18
West on Marine Drive

ERICKSON PLAYFIELD......23
Fourth and Race St.

FIERO MARINE
LABORATORY.........................18
City Pier, Foot of Lincoln
452-9277, Ext. 272

FIRST STREET HAVEN..........15
107 E. First
457-0352

FLAGSTONE MOTEL............13
415 E. First
457-9494

FOOTHILL POETRY
SERIES...22
Peninusla College
452-9277

GLEN MAR BED AND
BREAKFAST................................13
318 N. Eunice
457-4686

GRAYLINE TOURS.................18
1423 E. Fourth
457-4140

GREENERY.................................14
117 E. First
457-4112

GREYHOUND BUS
DEPOT.....................................11
215 N. Laurel
452-7611

HAGUEWOOD'S...............15
221 N. Lincoln
457-0424

HARBOR GALLERY............20
Harbortowne Mall
222 N. Lincoln
457-1853

HARBOR HOUSE
BED & BREAKFAST
139 W. 14th
457-3424

HICKORY DOCK...............15
128 W. Railroad
457-0542

HILL HAUS MOTEL...........13
111 E. Second
452-9285

JURY'S INN.............................15
110 E. Railroad
452-1139

LA CASITA.............................15
203 E. Front
452-2289

LINCOLN PARK.........14, 23
1943 W. Lauridson
457-0411

MAKAH MUSEUM..................19
Neah Bay
645-2711

M & C TAVERN........................22
116 W. Front
457-9971

ODYSSEY BOOKSHOP.......21
114 W. Front
457-1045

OLYMPIC NATIONAL PARK
VISITORS CENTER.................22
South on Race Street
452-9235

PEDAL 'N PACK.......................23
120 E. Front
457-1240

PENINSULA COLLEGE
1502 E. Lauridsen
452-9277

PENINSULA FILM
SOCIETY......................................22
c/o Odyssey Bookshop
457-1045

PENINSULA GOLF CLUB...23
105 Lindberg Road
457-7348

PISCES SEAFOODS................16
201 W. Railroad
452-8261

PORT ANGELES BOAT
HAVEN......................................23
West on Marine Drive
452-4444

PORT ANGELES
COMMUNITY
PLAYHOUSE......................21
Liberty and E. Lauridsen
452-6651

PORT ANGELES FINE ART
CENTER....................................20
1203 E. Eighth
457-3532

PORT ANGELES HIGH
SCHOOL
AUDITORIUM....................21
1304 E. Park

PORT ANGELES
LIGHT OPERA......................21
457-7912

PORT ANGELES
SPEEDWAY.............................23
East on Hy. 101

PORT ANGELES
SYMPHONY..........................21
452-7300

RED LION
BAYSHORE
INN...13
221 N. Lincoln
452-9215

Vancouver

Roll On, Columbia!

As the oldest continuous settlement in Washington, Vancouver occupies a special place among the state's cities. Some of the oldest remnants from white incursions into the region can be found here: an apple tree planted in 1826; a log cabin still standing from the late 1830s. So, too, can reminders of the methods used to subdue the wildness of the place be seen in the restoration of the original fort and trading post alongside which the city grew up

The Columbia River must have been an impressive sight to those early travelers and traders. It was the route between the interior and commerce by sea, as they knew it. But what a highway! Water from that entire great basin, from watersheds in the northern Rockies, gouging its way through that narrow slot we know as the Columbia Gorge. The salmon and mighty sturgeon had used this tumultous highway for eons, and their hunters had run whole networks of culture from the coast well into the interior plains. For the people who came here traveling that highway from the inland meant literally shooting rapids, and until the age of steam going upstream meant portages. Vancouver was the port of call for both transport by sea and also commerce with the inland territory. Photos from the early days of steamboat shipping on the Columbia can be seen at the Historical Museum.

Its strategic location has meant for Vancouver a continued military presence as well, a presence which, along with a devastating epidemic, in the early days very quickly subdued one of the mightiest Northwest Indian nations, the Chinooks. Much of the history to be read here has military trappings and overtones, from the despotic control the Hudson's Bay Company's John McCoughlin held over early settlement, to the Navy shipyard town the place became during World War II.

But without strategic importance, Vancouver couldn't help being overwhelmed by the commercial and cultural dominance of nearby Portland. When the military reserve was decommissioned in 1947, Vancouver became increasingly a place of history. The trim fields and elegant Victorian houses have become an extensive museum complex with the original Fort Vancouver the focus of a project in post-settlement archeology.

Another factor in shaping contemporary Vancouver was the highway, and the car. When the ferry crossed the river from downtown Vancouver, and even after the river was bridged in the Teens, land and water traffic kept meeting here and kept the town active. But hedged as it is by the river, the military reserve and the industrial port, Vancouver could not really grow enough to withstand the freeway and the growth of suburbia. That Vancouver thrives as it does is proof of the endurance of communities. Whether the shock of growth and change can be overcome in a rebirth of this inner city seems doubtful, although efforts diligently go on. What remains are small treasures for the archeologist of the150 years just past.

ARRIVALS

Coming into Vancouver on I-5 from the north there is a zone of freeway rush that operates just north of the bridge, where the driver has trouble not zipping pell mell into Oregon. To see the city rather than just the tops of a couple of newer buildings, leave the freeway at West Fourth Plain Boulevard and drive a couple of blocks west to Main Street. You may then drive sedately south on Main Street, jogging a block to the right when you hit a rather annoying network of one-way streets downtown. Jog right, continue south, jog left at 5th Street and you're ready for a quick look at Main Street USA.

If you arrive from the south it's just as easy to find yourself flying through the suburban hinterlands. I would follow the same route as if coming from the north: exit at West Fourth Plain Boulevard and drive west to Main.

If you're arriving by car from either direction, it's very convenient to stop at the **Tourist Information Center** for a map of historic sites you'll be visiting.

The **Greyhound Bus Depot** puts you a little to the west of my arbitrary starting point, and if you land from a **Tri-Met** intercity bus at the transfer plaza, you are a couple of blocks closer in. **Amtrak** serves the city, with two arrivals each day from the north and south, at the old Vancouver Station, built in 1907 and one of the few depots of its size and period still open in the Northwest.

A QUICK LOOK

At the corner of Fifth and Main stands the **Evergreen Hotel**, a national historic building now in the process of restoration and renovation. And across the street the treble-arched monument at **Waterfront Park** and beyond that the freeway, demonstrating what a profound impact it has had on downtown Vancouver. Looking around you can see that the heart has really been knocked out of the city. Several of the older buildings are salvageable, but the overlay of uninspired building combined with the devastation of the Interstate make it hard to see what might restore the heart of this city. Up Main you can see the results of a fair amount of redevelopment, and newer financial institutions give some hint as to what drives the town, and from what quarter saving the look of the place might come. But the effects of gambling (a blight even on some of the attractive buildings), neglect and lack of coordinated planning have let the place go beyond the deterioration seen in most towns. And what do you do about the brewery? I thought maybe a Cambodian Buddhist monastery.

To your north, up Main Street, you will find most of the urban amenities of the place; west at Sixth takes you to Esther Short Park and several interesting things to see and do; if you turn east from Main onto Evergreen Boulevard you will pass several notable buildings along a tree-lined street, cross over I-5 (maybe they could put a lid on it, like Seattle is doing), and find yourself in the Fort Vancouver complex. With only a few exceptions most of the attractions of Vancouver are to be found roughly within the limits of these thoroughfares.

I like Main Street, Vancouver, a lot, and I've walked long stretches of it several times. When it was young, and rich, and newly paved Vancouver must have been quite a place. Looking at it now requires recognizing the space limits, so you don't get lost out there in the suburbs, then ferreting the interesting and attractive out of stretches of fairly dreary buildings.

PLACES TO STAY

I've stayed in motels out on East 78th and beyond, and never seen Vancouver at all, just as I've determined to get off the freeway downtown and found myself on the bridge more than once. So now I don't experiment. Now that I know how to get to the center, I then drive north on Main or Columbia, turn east on 12th Street and go directly to the **Shilo Motel**, part of a chain of motels which, aside from being fairly new and very quiet, has one attractive feature: the south-facing rooms look out over the old Providence Academy. It's one of the nicest urban views from a motel room that I know of. Meetings and small conventions seem to gather at the **Red Lion Inn at the Quay**, where you can get rooms overlooking the Columbia, and there's a good restaurant with a view of the river. Trouble is, it's self-contained enough, and just far enough removed, that you tend not to get out and about the town.

PLACES TO EAT

If you are in search of the historical as well as a fine meal, then you owe it to yourself to dine at **Hidden House**, in the mansion of the Hidden estate, built in 1870. The interior of the house is a museum well preserved, and the dining is from the freshest and sometimes most unusual the Columbia and the Pacific have to offer. On nice summer evenings you can eat on the deck and stroll around what remains of the estate.

Mentioned above is the **Red Lion Inn**, where the restaurant works diligently at providing an extensive menu of fresh seafood. The view of the river here is superb and is the only view restaurant in the area.

There are restaurants in other interesting environments. On the grounds of the Providence Academy is **Century House**, a convenient place for a lunch if you're on a walking tour, since it's in between downtown and Fort Vancouver, and it's across from the Shilo Motel. A short distance out on Main Street, in another mansion from the early days, is **Casa Grande** where the homey cooking and setting combine for a nice evening of dining.

A couple of downtown places, where you can rub elbows with the townsfolk are **The Holland Restaurant**, a longtime local favorite for traditional American fare; and **Dylan's**, filled at lunchtime with nearby office workers, a good place for a burger if you get into the back part, past the walkup frozen yoghurt counter.

The frozen yoghurt bar is good to know about if you're in need of a snack, as is **Coffeeville USA** across the way, where there are a couple of tiny tables and an espresso bar.

SEEING THE SIGHTS

The first thing I would do before having a closer look at Vancouver is stop by the **Tourist Information Center** or the **Chamber of Commerce** for the current tour map of parks and historic sites-- the route is growing and being developed, so the map changes. Unless you're a diligent walker, you won't want to try to hit all the sites on foot. The map shows the locations, and you can pick shorter segments out of the longer route.

Here is a relatively short cross-town walk that will give you a glimpse of what's left of old Vancouver. You can start at either end, and if you alter your return path, you'll encounter most of the interesting buildings. Start at **The Academy**. Built in 1873 as the Catholic Providence Academy, the buildings and grounds are in an excellent state of preservation, now house offices and shops, so you can wander through the main building. Don't miss seeing the small ornate chapel on the third floor, a genuine period piece now used for weddings.

Walk across to Main on any street-- I like zigzagging as a way of seeing the unexpected, for example, the minimalist art deco **Kiggins Theatre** or the novel toad tree stump sculpture at the corner of 11th. At Main, walk north to 13th for a look at Hidden House, then continue on around the block to see the rest of this complex of Victorian buildings. Despite the defacement along Main, this block is one of the most visually interesting in town.

At this point you may want to stroll Main Street a bit farther, say as far as the former Carnegie Library, now the Clark County Historical Museum. This was once the urban ideal: tree-line boulevards, shops and fine homes intermingled, the library close at hand. If you continue south from the Hidden Estate on Columbia, you will pass the Gothic brick **Saint James Church**, built in 1885, with its towers and unusual windows. Inside you can have a look at the altar, hand-carved in oak.

A few more blocks south along Columbia and you come to the corner of **Esther Short Park**, a four-square-block concentration of several of Vancouver's more notable visual attractions. Built on the site of one of the earliest homesteads, the park land was deeded to the city by that important pioneer family who established the original townsite. Within the park grounds are two memorial statues, one to the pioneer woman and the other, a mighty totem, to the river's original people. Other attractions are a steam locomotive, two immense millstones brought round the Horn (sculpture in their own right), a playground, and the beautiful and well-preserved Slocum House, built in 1867 for the famous sailor, now a community theatre.

If you care to extend your walk, you can strike out for the port and industrial district to the west. Along the way you will come upon the 1907 **Vancouver Station**, still in use by Amtrak. On your return try to visualize some new use for the brewery. How did it ever get built so close in?

PARKS

If you are back at your starting point near The Academy, you can walk east along Evergreen Boulevard and, crossing the freeway, enter a region of large parks that grace Vancouver. Because of the distances, you may want to go by car, or catch C-Trans Bus on Evergreen Boulevard so you don't have the long hikes from place to place. Evergreen is the former Officers' Row, a line of Victorian dwellings running along the upper margin of **Fort Vancouver Park**. Many of these buildings are in ongoing use as private residences; one, once used by Ulysses S. Grant, is now a museum; another, Marshall House, one of the finest on the row, has been lovingly restored and for awhile was a restaurant. A walk along this tree-lined street makes a quiet and pleasant stroll. Notice the bandstand on the lawn near the street, where often you can hear concerts in the summer.

Evergreen Boulevard leads to the National Park Service Museum and Interpretive Center, and from there you are led to the reconstruction of the Hudson's Bay Company post. The broad expanses of lawn left from the military reserve make for good picnicing, and the empty barracks and other abandoned buildings lend a kind of stillness out of time; below you the river continues along. Unfortunately the serenity is somewhat marred by Pearson Air Park, directly below. However, if you have a yen to fly, you can take an air tour of Mt. St. Helens with **Vancouver Air**. Below the Air Park, along the river, you'll find **Marine Park**, with its playing fields and boat access.

Another park complex lies north of Evergreen Blvd, along Fort Vancouver Way. This system, called **Central Park,** includes the former military hospital, now Barnes General Hospital, Clark College and City College, with grounds and recreational facilities, and **Marshall Park** , where you'll find a recreation center and indoor swimming pool. At the northern edge of this complex, near the corner of Fourth Plain Boulevard and T Street, stands the oldest apple tree in the state, said to have been planted sometime between 1826-29, under the direction of old factor McLoughlin himself. Yet another addition to the complex, **Waterworks Park** is the place where many outdoor concerts are held in the summer, at the amphitheatre there.

At the northern edge of what were once Vancouver's city limits, **Leverich Park** offers a number of recreational facilities, a stadium, called Kiggins Bowl, and plenty of space and shady spots for walking and picnicing. Burnt Bridge Creek runs through the park, creating a setting a little more like wilderness than most urban parks. Also in this park you will find **Covington House**, the oldest pioneer house in the state, built in the mid 1840s and moved here in the 1930s from its original site a mile or so north.

MUSEUMS & GALLERIES

Of all the historical collection, restorations and reconstructions around Vancouver, my favorite is the **Clark County Historical Museum**. Housed in the former Carnegie Library, the museum has a welcoming feeling to it. A giant cottonwood enfolds much of the red brick structure, descendent of the original tree that marked Lewis and Clark's landing in 1805. Tiny humorous prehistoric carved rock statues guard the entrance, a play on the stone lions outside grander structures. Inside, the place is packed with memorabilia, and if some of the exhibits seem a bit static, their quality of being frozen in time is tempered by the sheer quantity of unusual and intriguing objects, and the quality of their presentation. The museum displays special and traveling exhibits as well.

Equally intriguing for its assemblage of early artifacts is the reconstruction of the **Hudson's Bay Company Stockade** at Fort Vancouver. Several original buildings, most notably the Chief Factor's residence, have been reconstructed and filled with furnishings, tools, clothing and other objects depicting daily life here in the 1850s. Reconstructions include a carpenter shop, a blockhouse complete with cannon, and a cookhouse and bakery. Volunteer guides make the exhibits and the history come alive for the visitor, and on autumn evenings, guides and actors present a "living museum" by candlelight, in which many of the fort's daily activities can be seen in action.

An instructive beginning to this rather lengthy historical tour is the **National Park Service Interpretive Center**, which explains much of the background of exploration up the Columbia and the fur trade generally. A playground and picnic tables make this a good place to let the kids loose, or just sit and watch Mt. Hood brooding on the eastern horizon.

The third historical exhibit at Fort Vancouver is the **Ulysses S. Grant Museum**, in the oldest house (1849) along Officer's Row. Grant, then a brevet major, served a tour of duty here in 1852-53, and the museum contains much Grant memorabilia as well as other articles from the Civil War period.

Art galleries don't abound in Vancouver, probably the effect of the nearness of Portland, but you can see exhibits of paintings and other works in several places around town. The **Geme Gallery** holds on downtown, and there is a small exhibit space for local work at the **Uptown Gallery** in the

Main Street Florists. The **Index Gallery** at Clark College offers a lively program of visiting exhibits, as well as occasional student shows.

Periodic exhibits of work by area artists are held at the **Columbia Arts Center**, where many performing arts events are held as well. And, if you want to hunt around, you can see regional art at the **Vancouver Memorial Hospital** and at **St. Joseph's Community Hospital**.

A NIGHT OUT

Because it's such a vast bedroom community, restaurants and clubs with entertainments are spread out all over the place. If you're looking for some specific kind of nightlife, I suggest you check the Friday edition of the Columbian, where there is a thorough listing for live entertainment both here and in Portland. I mentioned the **Columbia Arts Center** above. The center is a former church converted to multiple cultural purposes, where you'll find many of the performing arts events that go on in Vancouver throughout the year, both local and traveling productions.

Among the several musical organizations performing in Vancouver and vicinity is the **Columbia Symphony**, an orchestra made up of some of the top regional players, which appears occasionally as part of the **Music Arts Series** at the Columbia Arts Center. Another active group is the **Vancouver Brahms Singers**, appearing frequently at different auditoriums around town. Throughout the summer two music series while away the hours, one at noon on Fridays in the 9th Street Plaza at 9th and Broadway, the other on Friday evenings in Waterworks Park.

Community theatre is lively in Vancouver. The

Old Slocum House in Esther Short Park has a resident theatre company performing several productions throughout the year. The **Tears of Joy Theatre** bases its work on puppetry and plays for kids (the group sponsors the annual International Children's Festival) but often stretches itself into other dramatic performances. The community troupe **Encore Players** keeps one play or another in production pretty much the year 'round, with performances at the Arts Center or Slocum House.

If you're just out for a night on the town, you can get easy-listening rock music weekends at the Red Lion and at **Stuart Anderson's Cattle Co.** Other places nearby are the lounge at **The Crossing**, a kind of piano-bar atmosphere, and, for old rock 'n' roll memories and Chinese food in the heart of town, **Eden Gate** can supply both on Friday and Saturday nights. Some of the better-known regional groups play **The Sports Page**, but you'll need your car or a bus to get out there.

SPORTS

The readiest access to a variety of sports activities is at the recreation center in **Marshall Park,** part of the Central Park complex. Here you'll find an indoor swimming pool and a wide variety of other facilities. At nearby City College Park you'll find a fitness course and adjacent to that, tennis courts at Clark College. The city operates tennis and racquetball courts at the **Vancouver Tennis and Racquetball Center**, a highly-rated indoor facility.

The public is welcome at the **Green Meadows Golf Course**, and there is a ball and soccer field at **Marine Park**, where there is also access to the river for fishing and boating, etc.

If square dancing is your sport, there's an active scene around Vancouver. Check the schedules at the **Clark County Square Dance Center**.

BIG EVENTS

A selection of annual events around Vancouver starts off in January with the **Clark College Jazz Festival**, an all-day affair held in the gym, culminating in a kind of battle of the bands in the evening. In March, the **Vancouver Festival of Dance** is held over several days at different locations around town. Later in the spring, the **Society of Washington Artists** holds its annual exhibit. competition and sale, in the middle of May. Late June brings the city's extravagant **Fort Vancouver Days**, two weeks of a wide variety of events culminating in the annual Fourth of July celebration, with fireworks, at Fort Vancouver Park. During the festivities you can see and be part of river-related events like saiboat and rubber raft racing, eating events like the great chili cook-off, rodeos and dances. Also part of the festival is the annual **Artworks** arts and crafts show, held on the grounds at Fort Vancouver.

In mid-September St Joseph's Church School sponsors the annual **Vancouver Sausage Fest** as a fund raiser, and in October the city celebrates its oldest citizen at the **Old Apple Tree Festival**, held in the park around the tree-- incidentally, this tree is now 160 years old and still bears fruit. Not bad. And to end the year, in mid-December there's a Christmas celebration at Fort Vancouver.

This is only a part of the many events going on throughout the year; a complete schedule is available from the **Visitors Bureau.**

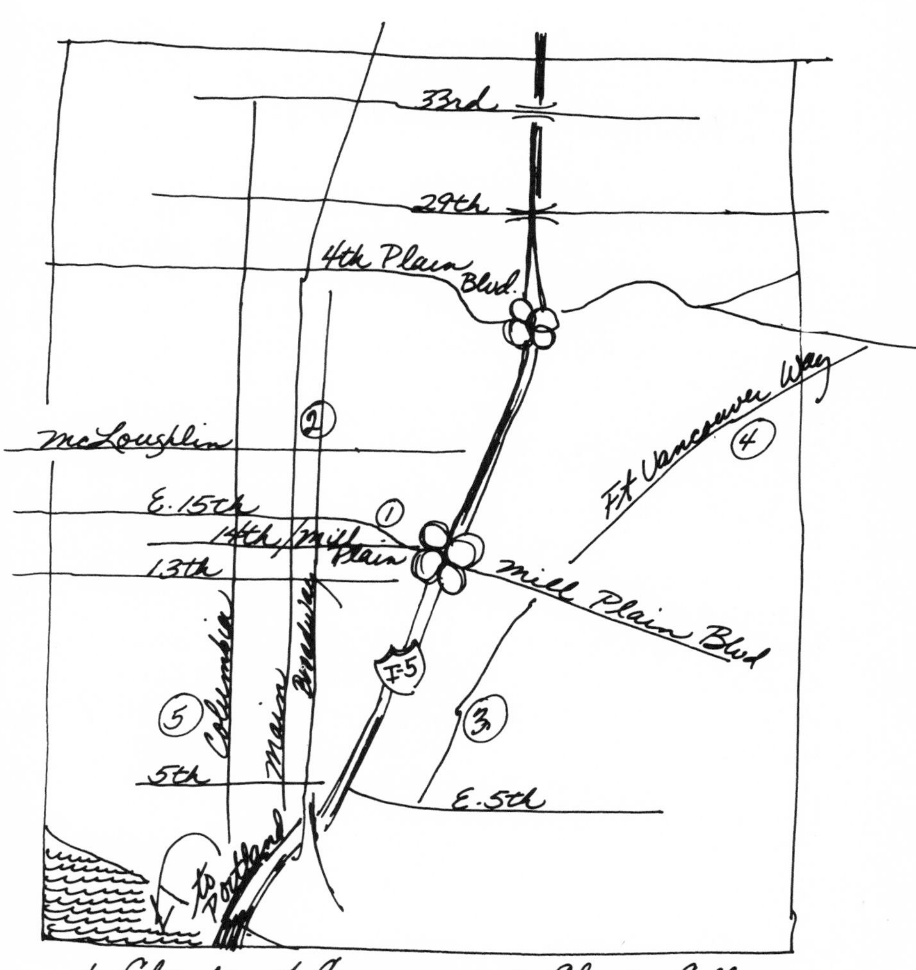

1. Chamber of Commerce
2. Museum
3. Fort Vancouver
4. Clark College
5. Esther Short Park

Downtown Vancouver.

Vancouver Index

ESTHER SHORT PARK....38
Columbia between Sixth and Eighth
696-8171

FORT VANCOUVER........39
Evergreen Blvd.
696-7655

FORT VANCOUVER DAYS & INDEPENDENCE DAY CELEBRATION.........40
1105 E. Fifth
693-5481 or 694-2588

GEME ART GALLERY........41
209 W. Sixth
693-7772

GREEN MEADOWS GOLF COURSE....................43
N.E 78th at NE 72nd Ave.
256-1510

GREYHOUND BUS DEPOT...........................34
512 Columbia
696-0186

HIDDEN HOUSE RESTAURANT......................36
100 W. 13th
696-2847

HOLLAND RESTAURANT......................36
Main and McLoughlin
694-7842

HUDSON'S BAY COMPANY............................41
Fort Vancouver Stockade
696-7655

INDEX GALLERY.................42
Clark College
699-0305

INTERNATIONAL CHILDREN'S FESTIVAL
Waterworks Park
695-3050

KIGGINS THEATER...........37
1011 Main
695-5141

LEVERICH PARK.................40
39th and M
696-8171

MARINE PARK.............39, 43
S. Portco Drive
696-8171

MARSHALL PARK......39, 43
1009 E. McLoughlin
Pool: 696-7946
Info: 693-4263

MUSIC ARTS SERIES..........42
696-7143

FORT VANCOUVER NATIONAL HISTORIC SITE....................39
1501 E. Evergreen Blvd.
696-7655

OLD APPLE TREE FESTIVAL......................44
Columbia Way at I-5
696-7655

PARKS AND RECREATION DEPARTMENT
696-8171

PEARSON AIRPARK
696-8191

RED LION INN............35, 36
100 Columbia
694-8341

ST. JAMES CHURCH.........38
218 W. 12th
693-3052

ST. JOSEPH'S COMMUNITY HOSPITAL.............................42
600 NE 92nd Ave.
256-2142

SAUSAGE FESTIVAL.........44
St. Joseph's Church
6500 Highland Drive
695-8666

SHILO MOTEL.....................35
401 E. 13th
696-0411

SLOCUM HOUSE..............43
Esther Short Park
W. Sixth and Esther St.

SLOCUM HOUSE THEATER.................................38
W. Sixth and Esther St.
695-5762

SOCIETY OF WASHINGTON ARTISTS..................................44
574-2183

SPORTS PAGE......................43
8052 E. Mill Plain Blvd.
694-2519

STUART ANDERSON'S..43
415 E. 13th
695-1506

TEARS OF JOY THEATER.................................39
695-3050

TENNIS AND RACQUETBALL CENTER..................................39
NE Stapleton Rd. at E. 18th
696-8123

ULYSSES S. GRANT MUSEUM...............................41
1106 E. Evergreen Blvd.
694-4002

Clark County Historical Museum
-Vancouver-

Olympia
the Capital

There's no other view in Washington quite like the view of the state capitol at Olympia from the I-5 freeway, going either way. The capitol dome is nestled in a crown of trees, and there's no getting away from it-- the symbolism, especially for anybody who struggled (or dozed) through Washington State history in high school, is a subliminal shot of patriotism (or jingoism), not so much for the government image as for its visual association with our true dedication here, the false hemlock, the doug fir. And seeing that dome lit up at night, gosh. We'll come back to the capitol.

Being at the southern reach of Puget Sound Olympia also marks a kind of jumping-off place for Sound dwellers heading south-- for years we made trips rounding Budd Inlet and going west to Grays Harbor for the clams. South of Olympia the terrain changes, the great geologic outflow called southwest Washington, with its logging and small towns and farms.

But it wasn't until state government business took me there that I ever actually looked at Olympia (except for that lovely dome), and when I looked I found an inner city on the edge of rediscovery, with a lot of new zip revving up, while up the hill the business of government cruised slowly on.

Government has always been integral to Olympia, since the first custom house, and hence the first official port of entry on Puget Sound, was established on Budd Inlet in 1851. By 1854, Governor Stevens had arrived in the newly formed Washington Territory, Olympia had been named its Capitol, and the first Territorial Legislature had convened here. They fought a year-long Indian war here in 1859.

As with other cities, the forests built the town. Log shipping, lumber, wood products, mills dotted the shores of the South Sound, with Olympia as the leading port. Today, Olympia is still an important port of call. Logs and log products still swing onto ships in the harbor, and exotic remnants of former industry can be seen around Budd Inlet.

Olympia, like other cities, suffered from suburban sprawl, and perhaps from the innate conservatism of government, and the effects are still being felt. However, the growth of The Evergreen State College has inserted an inherently progressive element that can be seen in many ways, especially downtown. It's a community residents are immensely proud of, and the community has generally responded to the needs of an emerging city core wholeheartedly.

ARRIVALS

When driving to Olympia there are several approaches off I-5 from either direction, but I suggest you leave the freeway at Exit 104, which devolves smack in front of the Capitol campus. Approaches from the east or west will lead you to the same place. You turn north on Capitol Way to cover pretty much the limits of this visit. You branch out around Capitol Lake and the Inlet, but much of what you see lies between the campus and the water and the several blocks either side of Capitol Way. At this first intersection you encounter, there is a **Visitor Information Center** open when the Legislature is in session, to keep in mind when you visit the capitol grounds or as a start to your tour.

There is no commercial airline service directly to the **Olympia Airport**, but the field is used extensively by charter services and private planes. If you do land there, you can rent a beater from the charter service **Pearson Air.** A cab trip from the airport to downtown Olympia via **Red Top Taxi** costs $5.50. If you're traveling on a scheduled airline you can land at the Seattle-Tacoma International airport and reach Olympia (a 65-mile trip) on the **Capitol Airporter** at a cost of about $17.

Both **Greyhound** and **Trailways** bus systems serve Olympia, but since the downtown Greyhound Depot closed not long back, riding the bus here just isn't the same. I liked stepping out of the depot across the street from Sylvester Park within sight of the old capitol building and walking distance of restaurants and motels. The depot even maintained its lunch counter (a classic) right up till the end.

If you're cruising the inland waters, there are several marinas along both shores of Budd Inlet. **Percival Landing Park** is a public dock right at the foot of Budd Inlet with 3-day moorage facilities with showers, power and easy access to downtown Olympia.

GETTING AROUND

A car isn't the hindrance in Olympia that it can be in some towns and cities: parking is easy downtown, and the layout of streets including the one-ways, is pretty orderly and logical. Because all crosstown traffic is funneled onto the bridge between Capitol Lake and Budd Inlet at 4th Avenue, the one-way thoroughfares State and 4th get a lot of traffic. But it really is a walker's town, and a cyclist's town, too (you can rent bikes at **Olympic Outfitters**). While there are some steep hills around Capitol Lake, the rise to the capitol campus is a gentle one, and most of the interesting walking or biking excursions are along the water. Bus service is excellent. **Intercity Transit** serves Olympia and the adjacent cities of Lacey and Tumwater, and environs. On working visits I've used my car for a few side trips-- Tumwater Park, the west side, Priest Point Park and the college-- but mostly I've left it at the motel.

PLACES TO STAY

It's a great town for bed & breakfasts, though they don't seem to be on the rapid increase as they are in some places. Big, older homes around the Capitol, quiet tree-lined streets, walking distance to most attractions. **Unicorn's Bed & Breakfast** fills the bill. Another is called **Life Directions**, located in the same part of town.

For a downtown motel **Aladdin's Motor Inn** isn't bad, and it has the uncommon distinction of being connected to a top-rate restaurant, **Arnold's**: memorable breakfasts at 6:30; politicos and hotshots at lunch; fine cuisine at dinner. Across the way, the largeish **Governor's House Hotel** is the only remaining equivalent of the grand downtown hotels of the past; some rooms overlook Capitol Lake.

On the west side of Capitol Lake, high on the ridge with a splendid prospect, the **Westwater Inn** is outside walking distance, but being out of the way it's quiet and the views are rewarding. Another place out on the edges, the **Tyee**, is said to be where much of the politicking goes on during the session, if you want to see how that game is played. I have a hunch all the motels and lounges and eateries are abuzz when laws are getting made and money spent.

For campers and RV travelers the closest facility I could find is **Deep Lake Resort**, a lakeside ground with hookups, tent spaces and cabins.

EATING OUT

If there's a place where fine cooking ought to prosper Olympia should be it, just because of all the free lunches that get spread around. And indeed the number of excellent, and interesting, restaurants is fairly high, a lot of styles represented.

Having become something of a collector of Carnegie Libraries around the state, I was gratified and amused to come upon **Carnegie's**, Olympia's

Carnegie Library, now in private hands and an ambitious restaurant. The library building is one of the finest I've seen, lovingly preserved and restored, and the bookcases and remaining volumes that line the walls make a decor worth seeing.

One of my favorite places, from the days of its old location near the campus, is **Crackers** which, when it moved, expanded into a great old building in the heart of the town renovation, and built up some of the ideas the owners had started on the hill. Crackers attracts the growing hip urban set that is making the town come alive. Nice place.

The oyster beds are famous, as has been said; the clams are like nowhere else. Serving this local bounty in the fine style is **Gardner's**, noted for its treatment of seafoods, pasta and sauces. The geoduck is worth the experience. Other fine dining establishments include, predictably, a mansion, in this case an early mayor's. **Seven Gables** has, besides a well-prepared and varied menu, a terrific view of Mt Rainier across Budd Inlet, Sunday brunches, and a veranda to enjoy it all from in nice weather.

A couple of restaurants with exceptional views should be noted. Built right out over the water on Budd Inlet, the **Ebb Tide** is especially pleasant if the view up the sound is clear. The menu is solid seafood and American fare. Overlooking Tumwater Falls, **Falls Terrace** combines an excellent view with modest prices to make it a very popular place.

My folks were always great fans of the **Olympia Oyster House**, so I went there and had a lesson in oysters, their sizes and varieties and flavors. The menu and the servers are very helpful in learning about the tiny Olympia Oyster and others that grow in the area. The smallest, freshest oysters to be had, lightly breaded and fried right, not bad.

On the ethnic side, the local choice in Chinese restaurants seems to be the **Chinatown**, with the kind of menu and quality cooking folks educated in the cuisine like to see. One of the special places that is lending the upbeat air to the new activity along 4th Avenue is **Barb's Soul Cuisine** where the cooking is more subtle than barbeque, but the barbeque sure smells good. And a list like this wouldn't be complete without mentioning the place where the locals hang out, the famous **Spar**. I think every town and city has a place like this, but they're not always renowned. Check it out.

It's good to know about a coffee house. The **Smithfield Cafe** is open early enough to be useful, has the cappucino you're longing for, as well as other espressos and coffees, and sweets and treats. The Smithfield, along with a couple of galleries, holds down the west end of the 4th Avenue district, giving it some purpose and definition. It's also good to know about the all-night **Bayview Deli**, right at the bottom of the Inlet in the Bayview Market,where you can get an espresso in a styro cup any time of the day or night.

SEEING THE SIGHTS

I'd organize my look at Olympia around the fact that this is the very farthest reach of salt water into the Puget Basin, or, if you will, the most distant watershed from the open sea, the bottom of the sound. And an excellent place to start out and get oriented is around a wonderful waterfront renewal project, **Percival Landing Park**. From this focal point (there are public restrooms here) you can trek outward to explore the reaches of Capitol Lake and the Deschutes River, both shores of Budd Inlet, the capitol on the hill, and the town nearby.

From the Landing round the Inlet heading west on 4th until you come to the bridge. The view all along this stretch can be stunning. Being from a more northerly place I find it unusual to view the Olympics from this perspective (Rainier too); traveling along the Inlet on either shore just heightens the respective views. You can understand why a community took hold here and grew up so quickly.

Looking south from the bridge you can see how you would follow Deschutes Parkway along the west side of Capitol Lake to explore the wonderful wetland areas and the tumbling mouth of the Deschutes River at Tumwater Falls Park. Stock up at the Bayview Deli right there at hand or plan a late lunch at Falls Terrace and you could make a full day of it.

Walking back along 4th Avenue (leaving the west side until later) at Columbia you enter a stretch of urban Olympia that is varied and interesting and, to my eye at least, forms a core of attractions illustrative of a reviving city. From the Smithfield coffee house on the west end to the exotic mural on the wall of the China Clipper Cafe on the east, with several beautiful restorations like the Wards Building and the Chambers Building at the corner of Capitol Way displayed in between, a trek along 4th makes a good beginning to a walking tour downtown. Continue this exploration by weaving the several blocks downtown to include the Washington Center for the Performing Arts, another important restoration project, and the **Old Capitol Building.** Built in 1891 and on the National Register of Historic Places, the Old Capitol is a remarkable example of stonework complete with gargoyles. Note Sylvester Park, and across the street the grand hotel **Olympian**, alas now apartments but you can visit the shops in what is left of the lobby, and the ballroom is still occasionally used for dancing.

These peregrinations have brought you back toward Capitol Way, and if you strike out up the hill you'll come to the **State Capitol Campus**, a tour by itself. When the Legislature's meeting you can hang around and hear what my friend calls the "hum of power." The capitol building is of course the big attraction, with its great dome and chandelier and marble stairs, plus the murals both visible and covered. But the grounds to the south are well worth seeing, especially the greenhouses where the plantings are nurtured. Also check out the Governor's Mansion, and the art and native authors collections in the State Library. It's worth taking the guided tour just to get a complete look at the place. Your walking tour should certainly extend a few blocks beyond the campus to the **State Capitol Museum**, housed in a stately mansion among big trees in a quiet neighborhood.

PARKS

Several of Olympia's notable parks have already been mentioned in passing. **Percival Landing Park** has the city marina for overnight moorages and a long wooden promenade that is a cross between a boardwalk and a working pier. The view of the harbor, shipping and the marina encourages that image. **Capitol Lake Park** occupies the perimeter of much of Capitol Lake, giving the city a kind of calm focus. The lake has unfortunately been recently found to be too polluted to swim in, and it is hoped that by the time you get to Olympia the problem will be corrected, because as a swimming and wading beach and play area, Capitol Lake Park is a vital focus of activity in the summer for the whole community. The largest park in the city is **Priest Point Park**, on the east shore of Budd Inlet a short distance north of downtown. You can picnic along the edge of the Sound here in a serene atmosphere of trees and quiet water.

I was really taken by **Tumwater Falls Park** and have been back there several times to scramble and stroll along the Deschutes River as it tumbles into the lake, watching the fish ladders and musing on the bridges over the falls. There's a pictorial museum here, and a restaurant. If you get tired of all the exploring you can walk up the hill and tour the **Olympia Brewing Company** where they will reward you at the end with a perfectly chilled brew or two. At the south end of the park is a nature trail through lakeshore wetlands for bird and animal watching and picnics on the higher grounds.

Small but by no means insignificant is **Sylvester Park**, the formal urban square under the trees with benches and statuary and plantings. There you can mellow out looking at the stately mass of the old capitol, and on certain summer days and evenings be graced with musical performances. The newspaper and posters around town have the times.

HISTORY AND ART

Mention has been made of the handsome **State Capitol Museum**. The grounds also deserve mention because of the intricate herb garden at the back, and along the sides a specimen collection of native plants that makes an instructive and absorbing walk. Inside the museum are excellent collections of Indian and pioneer history, as well as the history of state government.

At Tumwater Falls Park is **Henderson House**, a restored Victorian mansion housing a pictorial museum of regional history.

The many pieces that comprise the art collection at the state capitol are best seen by following the guided tour; they include murals by Tobey and Callahan in the State Library, and groups of paintings in the Capitol building that are both historic and controversial. There is also a quantity of interesting statuary on the campus.

Commercial galleries have sprung up with the renewed interest in the center of Olympia. **Marianne Partlow Gallery** is one of the established ones, showing local and regional artists. Nearby, the **Artists' Co-op Gallery** is a community of artists gathered to maintain a showplace for their work. These two galleries and the Washington Center, along with the historic buildings, shops and park at hand, form an attractive complex of things to see and do.

Another cooperative display gallery, this time for the useful arts, is **Cornerstone Pottery**. And at the west end of 4th Avenue are a couple of galleries that help give that corner its nice look. **Gallery 210 1/2** is an exhibit space for local artists sponsored by the Live Arts Foundation, a nonprofit community arts center. **Childhood's End** displays regional art and collectibles, and it provides the exhilerating whale mural on the Water Street wall.

SHOPPING

Many of the big department stores, the shoe stores and boutiques, have fled to the malls, and you can see the empty spaces they've left behind, which are hard to fill. What you find instead are small and unusual stores occupying the niches.Ideas for using those big commercial spaces will come in time. Meanwhile, if you like the process of shopping, have a look at the out-of-the-ordinary shops in the heart of town. One I like is **Archibald Sisters**, partly for the decor (the glass awning out front is eye-catching), and for the collection of zany gift items inside. Another unusual shop is **Earth Magic**, which sells crystals. Somehow looking at a collection of crystals is more compelling than costlier gems-- maybe it's because of the salutory properties that are supposed to accrue to crystals. I don't have a big listing for antiques, though there are a number of shops downtown. One place that looked like it might repay some serious browsing is **The Antiquerie**, a collection of hundreds of vases, bottles and small glass objects you wouldn't want to send a bull into.

One concentrated shopping and touring hit is the Wards Building. It's one of the first restorations of a downtown structure, and houses several shops and businesses. An interesting place in the Wards Building is **First Light Media**, which sells prints of historic photos by the early Olympia photographer Vibert Jeffers. And you can see Jeffers' original studio building, from 1903, at the corner of 5th and Washington.

Bookstores fill a surprising number of the niches in downtown Olympia. A couple of places selling used books are **Browser's Bookshop** for a paperback to read in the motel, and **At Home with Books,** which has a nice supply of new and used books. The **Fireside Bookstore** is not only a very pleasant place to seek out a new book, but it's in the lobby of the Hotel Olympian, so stopping there gives you a chance to have a look at that edifice.

A NIGHT ON THE TOWN

There's a kind of mellow business to the downtown streets evenings, which maybe comes from the concentration of cafes along 4th. The great number of events that go on at the **Washington Center for the Performing Arts** helps to focus cultural activity-- this important restoration and renovation project has, in the few years since it's been completed, been an important factor in the new vitality of the place. Among the music organizations performing in the space are the **Olympia Symphony Orchestra**, and, less frequently, its companion group, the **Olympia Area Youth Symphony**. Singing companies include the **Olympia Chorale** and the **Light Opera Company**.

One of the established residents of the thespian scene in Olympia is the **Capitol Repertory Theatre** which presents a full program of performances at its own house during the regular season, and a Shakespeare Festival in the summer. Another place to know about for live drama presentations is the **Olympia Little Theatre**, a community of players that perform several plays a year on its boards. There's a jazz scene here, too, and a good one according to reports. Check newspaper and bulletin boards for events in this fragile medium. I heard live jazz coming out of the air one sunny afternoon on 4th, some anonymous tenor person working through Monk's Well You Needn't.

If it's loud music you're after, a couple of spots downtown offer it on a regular basis. The handbills I saw around were for rock 'n' roll at the **Fourth Avenue Tavern** on weekends, and an assortment of styles presented at the **Rainbow Restaurant**. As mentioned before, most of the big motels have lounges attached, and most of them, like the **Tyee**, have entertainment, maybe dancing, even, on a regular basis, and tend to be jumping when the session's on.

There's a downtown movie theatre, too, the **State Theatre**, that seems to show pretty interesting first and early run films, and that keeps some traffic on the evening streets, especially weekends. While it's a little far away, the **Evergreen State College** has theatre performances and other public events, including a classic film series.

You might want to check out the ballroom dancing situation by calling the **Olympia Ballroom Association**, sponsors of dancing lessons and events in the grand ballroom of the Hotel Olympian.

INDOOR & OUTDOOR SPORTS

In the summer you can rent a sailing dinghy right there at the lakeside in Capitol Lake Park, and sail out under the lee of that marvelous forested bluff under the Capitol dome. To check out possible rentals for sailing on Budd Inlet contact **Fiddlehead Marina** just north of Percival Landing.

In a land of outdoor sports, one of the handiest places is one that equips a variety of sportspersons. **Olympic Outfitters** provides equipment, rentals and advice on a wide range of sports activities in the region within reach of Olympia. You can rent bicycles here.

Swimming outdoors is accessible at **Priest Point Park** and, hopefully, Capitol Lake. The public indoor pool is at the **YMCA**, along with a host of other facilities. Other indoor sports such as raquetball and indoor tennis are south of town at the **Tumwater Valley Racquet Club** where some courts are available to visitors. In this area you'll find the nearest golf course, **Tumwater Valley Golf Club**. Outdoor tennis courts closest to town are on the west side, at **Woodruff Park**.

BIG EVENTS

My favorite annual event in Olympia goes on all summer-- the weekend **Farmers' Market** held along Thurston Avenue just north of Percival Landing. When there's nothing going on up the hill the action centers around the bottom of Budd Inlet, and on those glorious sunny weekends the downtown streets, the Farmers' Market and that huge rambling shopping center **Yardbird's**, where half the stuff is displayed outside in nice weather, gives the place an ongoing festival air that's fun to walk around in. Another ongoing event during the summer is the series of Friday Noon concerts in Sylvester Park.

The big annual community event is **Capital Lakefair**, complete with a parade, the second week in July. At the end of July and early August the **Thurston County Fair** attracts thousands to the Fairgrounds. Intercity Transit Bus # 80 serves the Fair from downtown Olympia. Also at the end of July the **Capital City Marathon** draws not only crowds, but crowds of dedicated runners as well, in men's, women's and wheelchair divisions.

June brings the big-league **Olympus World Championship Rally** auto race to Tumwater, and part of the course roars through downtown Olympia streets.

At the end of summer the Labor Day **Harbor Days Festival** celebrates the city's maritime heritage with, among other attractions, tugboat races. Spring brings the **Wooden Boat Fair** and the opening day of yachting season, both very attractive if you're interested in boats and boating. Also in May, the **Tumwater Bluegrass Festival**, for those of you who follow the itinerant fiddlers, and the **Southwest Washington Art Show**.

Equestrian events throughout the year take place at **The Trails Arena** near the airport, kind of a mecca for horse lovers, with a restaurant, a lounge for country and western music, and RV hookups for the wranglers. In June the big event is the Midsummer Classic Arabian Show.

For precise schedules of community events throughout the year, call or write the **Visitors and Convention Bureau** for the three towns around Budd Inlet.

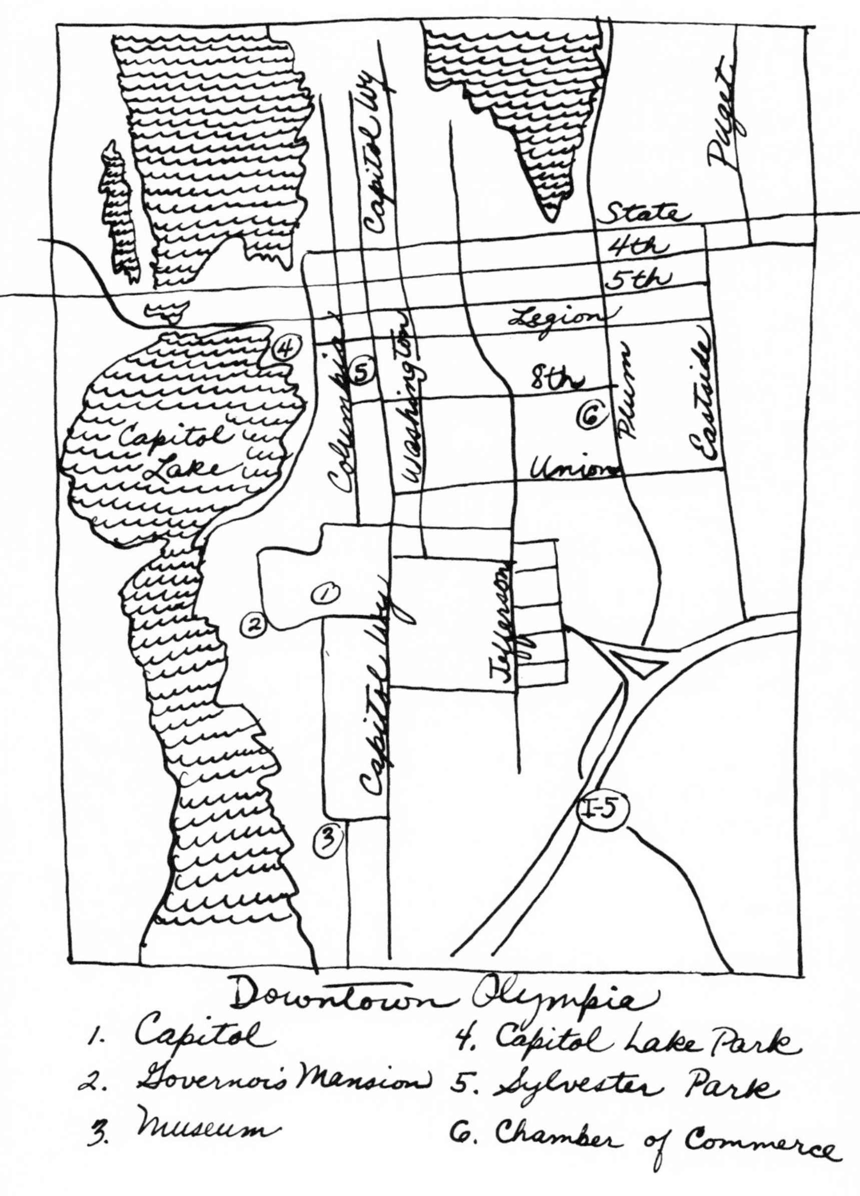

Downtown Olympia

1. Capitol
2. Governor's Mansion
3. Museum
4. Capitol Lake Park
5. Sylvester Park
6. Chamber of Commerce

Olympia Index

W.T. Preston — Stern wheel workboat; retired 1981.

Anacortes
On the Edge

That glacier, pushing at the sea, piling up till and rock, crushing and grinding away then retreating to expose promontories and clumps, built the San Juan and Gulf Islands, and where the great Skagit drainage pushed rich mud and topsoil on top of what was left, sculpted at the sea's edge, leaving a web of land and water where for centuries now, people have lived well off both worlds.

Cities along that edge are interesting because of the dual activity of working on land and working on water. In Anacortes, shipping docks, marinas and boatyards contrast with nearby forests and small farms, old residential streets and the commercial and industrial buildings downtown. Here there is a constant sense of the water near at hand. The bays, the channels and the islands are all part of nearly every view. On a peninsula that is actually Fidalgo Island, separated from the Skagit Valley by the Swinomish Channel that runs across its eastern side, Anacortes illustrates its history as a jumping-off place for work on the sea. Canneries, piers and boat moorages from the turn of the century are still standing and visible along the working waterfront. More recently, too, the land and sea connection has been made in the oil refineries taking advantage of the deep-water port to bring in crude by tanker; and off-shore oil rigs were recently built at Anacortes for barge shipment to Prudhoe Bay.

At its beginning, Anacortes had hopes (along with several other Puget Sound communities) of becoming the western terminus for the Northern Pacific Railroad, as it crept west in the late 1870s. That hope was shattered as were others along the way: the decline of the cod fishery, the decline of the town as a port, the retreat of the mills, and most recently the unrealized hopes of an industrial revival along the harbor to the east. What the visitor sees are remnants of this checkered history, and what remains of the fishery, log shipping and industry combine with the abandoned monuments of the past and the natural beauty of the setting to create scenes of very high visual interest.

ARRIVALS

Anacortes is the land side terminus of the **Washington State Ferry** system to the San Juan Islands, so as such, it is really a place of departures for most people, whether to get out to the islands, to Victoria, or on up to Alaska with the fishing fleet. And it is also a town oftentimes seen passing through; in the summer the lines of cars dragging through the downtown ferry route can be aggravating. Why not get out of the line, park the car and have a look? For many, in recent years, the possibility of doing just that has emerged with a park and ride system of shuttles from a municipal lot just off the first exit from Highway 20. That should make it easier to see Fidalgo along with the other islands, as well as help ease the excess ferry traffic.

The land side connection to the ferry is a spur off Highway 20, which connects with the Olympic Peninsula via Whidbey Island and the Keystone Ferry to Port Townsend. If you're a ferry nut there is a neat loop from Anacortes to Victoria to Port Angeles and back to Keystone, but you need a car or a bike to do it

The spur follows the main street of downtown Anacortes to 12th Street, then follows 12th west to Ship Harbor, the ferry terminal. If your only visit is along the ferry route, then you can still experience some of the interesting history of Anacortes by keeping your eyes open as you drive along above the Guemes Channel to the north. You will see shipyards and cannery buildings from the heyday of codfish processing. At the turn of the century all along this channel there were canneries, mills and factories, communities of Chinese laborers, and a population more than twice what it is today. If you're in luck you may see an oil tanker or log freighter, impressive sights in the narrow channel, or purse seiners demonstrative of Anacortes' ongoing connection with the sea. As you park at Ship Harbor notice the wetlands and relatively uncluttered beach, abandoned fisheries gone back to something of the days before Europeans, an area soon to become developed again, this time with condos, a marina, shops and even a native interpretive center.

But you should take the time to see Anacortes. Instead of turning left at 12th Street, drive straight on down Commercial Avenue to the Port Dock, and start from there. Do some exploring before you take off for the San Juans.

Arrival by public transportation is not so easy to do at Anacortes. The **Trailways Bus Line** runs to Anacortes and the Ferry every other day from Mount Vernon and Whidbey, so with some planning you can pursue a tour via public transportation. There are excellent walks in and around Anacortes, but since there is no transit system, your visit will be somewhat restricted. At the Anacortes Airport **West Isle Air** offers flights to and from the San Juans, but there is no commercial service between Anacortes and larger airports on the mainland. Area travelers often land at the Oak Harbor airport, served by **San Juan Airlines.** Anacortes based **Doug's Taxi**, serves the region's airports as well as the ferry terminal and towns in the valley, and offers sightseeing tours.

MARINAS

I first saw Anacortes from the deck of a purse seiner plying the inland waters out of Blaine, and I still think that's a special way to arrive at a place, even if it's not Singapore or Hong Kong. This is a port very definitely suited to travelers by boat: there are several excellent marinas, most necessary services are located nearby, and distances around town are not so great that exploration is uncomfortable on foot. Largest of the water-based services is **Cap Sante Boat Haven** operated by the Port of Anacortes. Overnight and short-term moorages are nearly always available and there are marine repair services and haulouts right at hand. A marine outfitter and a restaurant are right on the dock, and two large supermarkets are mere steps away.

Of the half dozen private marinas situated around the shores of Anacortes, all offer moorages and essential services to visitors. Locals have their favorites, but if you're only staying a night or two, it doesn't seem to make much difference. **Skyline Marina** on the west side of the island is quite a long distance from downtown, but as Skyline is something of a distinct community, you'll most likely find the services you need right at hand.

GETTING AROUND

The greater part of Anacortes was platted all at once (not true of most towns) in a neat grid, with lettered Avenues running north and south, and numbered Streets running east and west. When you enter Anacortes at the top of Commercial, you are at the southern end of what is actually P Avenue, the name of which was changed, according to some locals, because of its scatalogical connotations. Be that as it may, once you figure out that downhill is north, finding your way around should be simple.

Without a car, you are confined to the area you can walk in, unless you want to take Doug's Taxi.

Actually, you shouldn't find walking unpleasant since the older, interesting part of town is quite small and only rarely is the weather too rotten to get from place to place. You do need a car to get to the outlying parks and forest lands, unless you are an inveterate hiker.

PLACES TO STAY

As jumping-off place for the schedule-bound ferry system, Anacortes is better stocked with motels and other accomodations than many larger cities to serve people who have missed a boat. But the town rarely overflows with visitors, except perhaps during a couple of weekends in the summer, so it's easy to pick a place. My vote goes to the places with views, because the views are so grand here. One motel with good views that is also connected to a top-rate restaurant is **Islands Motel**. The restaurant, **La Petite**, is tiny as its name, caters mostly to the motel guests for breakfast and dinner, but takes reservations for its fine Dutch-based cuisine. Nearby, the **Anacortes Inn** has the same sweeping views of Mount Baker, Cap Sante and the islands, but without the restaurant.

Closer to the heart of town, and so more convenient for the several walking tours that follow, is **Cap Sante Inn**, the closest to a waterfront accomodation you'll find. Serviceable and convenient, especially to the Guemes Ferry bunch, the downtown **San Juan Motel** is the choice of several people I know who visit Anacortes regularly.

But the queen of restored downtown hotels anywhere, the splendid **White Gull Inn** is at this writing (early '87) alas not yet open. I break a rule of this book and include it (as I did the Davenport in Spokane) because if the White Gull is open by the time you get there, you should certainly consider taking a room. And if it isn't open yet you owe it to yourself to have a look at her at least, just for the quality of the restoration done to this building.

Other inns and bed & breakfast homes provide that family atmosphere so popular among weekenders in the Northwest. Again, views, and to some extent architecture, make some places notable. Along the ferry route, the **Channel House** has rooms looking north across the Guemes Channel. The **Nantucket Inn** in an archtypical Anacortes frame building just as you drive into town, looks down the broad slope across town and waterfront and islands north and east. In a quiet part of town overlooking the bay, **Dutch Treat House** is a big cheerful place where you could stash away a family for a weekend. Bed 'n' Breakfast conditions apply to these hostelries.

Campers will find **Washington Park** an excellent introduction to Anacortes. Occupying the western point of the island, the park's woods and beach walks provide good examples of island ecology, within walking distance of the ferry and a short drive from downtown. The park is suited to tent campers as well as RVs, and is especially handy for folks trailering boats. Reservations are advised. Less woodsy but out among the yachting set, **Skyline RV Park** has hookups and access to a variety of services at the marina.

PLACES TO EAT

The number of notable eateries in Anacortes is not large-- only **La Petite** is mentioned by the critics, and the Dutch cuisine is definitely worthy of note. It is a small place (hence the name) and reservations for dinner are advised. If you happen to stay the night at the adjacent Islands Motel, you may also be the lucky recipient of one of La Petite's fine breakfasts.

Other dining spots include **Slocum's** at Flounder Bay, with a view of Skyline Marina, and seafood specials that are fresh, well-presented and often unusual. Slocum's also provides a chowder bar and Sunday brunch. Another restaurant with a view, this time of the working port along the Guemes Channel, is **Boomer's Landing**. From almost any table, you can watch the activities of the log yard and freighters, fishing- boat building and repair, and occasionally a kingfisher or heron hunkered up in the rain. At the city's Cap Sant Marina you can dine at **Captain Speedy's**, a seafood place thrown in among the working boats, pleasure boats, Coast Guard station and marine outfitters, making dinner a nice appendage to a walk and exploration among things nautical.

If you're out with a gang of kids, or a bunch of big hungry tummies, I can recommend the burgers at the **International Bank of Gourmet Hamburgers** and the **Spaghetti Bread & Wine Co**. Tucked in among the alleyways behind an old bank building, this combination lunch and dinner place is reliable for solid fare.

At lunchtime you have an opportunity to see an interesting cross-section of the community at **Gere-a-Deli**, where workers from the boatyards rub elbows with the uptown professionals. Busy, upbeat and jovial, with interesting things to eat, it's a place to get to know some of the people of

Anacortes in a casual way. Another longtime dining institution in Anacortes is the Mexican place next to the Post Office, **El Jinete**.

For an early breakfast **The Best Little Restaurant in Town** opens at 6 am, with extremely nice people to wake up to. It's the Trailways bus stop, too. An early-morning meeting spot for locals is **Kate's**, which, though not open until 7 am, serves a homemade wholewheat cinnamon roll worth waiting for. There are no all night joints in downtown Anacortes.

Treats are things one likes to be able to find in a hurry, and right downtown, across from the Post Office, there is an irresistible place for treats, chocolate, ice cream and good coffee. **Sweet 'n' Sassy** sells regionally famous Boehme's candies, as well as a fudge and nut covered ice cream bar that's pretty extravagant.

SEEING THE SIGHTS

To get a quick look at Anacortes you can take the scenic drive, which will give you a broad view of the town and the island, including the spectacular vistas as seen from Cap Sante, Fidalgo Head and Mount Erie. Pick up the blue and orange signs along R Avenue (the first exit off Highway 20 as you come into town) and follow the loop that extends out to Washington Park along the Guemes Channel, runs through the Skyline development on a back road out to the mountain, and back into town. Along this route you see almost all the best public views of the Sound, the islands and the Cascades, and it's a good quick introduction to the beautiful surroundings and layout of the place.

Or, you can take one or more of several walks

around town that give you a closer, more leisurely, picture of the place but without the spectacular views (you really do need a car for those). A short walking tour begins along the lower (northern) end of Commercial Avenue. Start at Fifth and Commercial and walk north along Commercial all the way to the Port Dock, then turn east for two blocks to the bottom of R Avenue. Sights along the way include the newly restored White Gull Inn, as well as one or two other turn of the century buildings restored or in good condition. Also of interest are Marine Supply and Hardware, a commercial hardware in operation since 1909 that is a museum in itself, and boatbuilding operations ranging from handcrafted wooden sailing and rowing boats at the restored Freya Boatworks building on 3rd, to the sleek steel purseseiners built by Dakota Creek. The port warehouses and dock, commercial marinas, and the log export yard round out this tour of maritime Anacortes, old and new. Walking south along R Avenue, you will come to the restored Burlington Northern train depot, now the offices of the **Anacortes Arts and Crafts Foundation** and focus of the annual street fair. The Depot is also the permanent home of the **Anacortes Steam Railway**, a delightful narrow-gauge replica of the elegant age of steam trains, with cars done in plush, brass and polished woods. During the summer months the train runs on its bit of track every weekend, and thousands ride on it every year. The third attraction in this collection of memorabilia is the sternwheeler **W.T. Preston**, now landbound in its retirement from pulling snags up and down Puget Sound and open for visits during the summer. To finish your walk you can hike on along the shore of Cap Sante Boat Haven or go west on 7th back to Commercial, noticing the two restored commercial buildings at the corner of 7th and Commercial and at 6th and Commercial across the street.

If the weather is fine, and you'd like a more ambitious hike, one with a completely different perspective on the town, start downtown at 5th and Commercial and follow a zigzag path of residential streets and interesting old houses to the corner of 7th and N. There you'll find one of the town curiosities, **Causland Park**, with its intricate if somewhat outlandish rockwork. Skirting the park puts you at the corner of 8th and M, and on the opposite corner you'll see the **Anacortes Museum**, originally a Carnegie Library now restored and housing some good collections, especially of old photographs. You might also want to backtrack to7th and M to see the Episcopal Church, built in 1896.

Follow 8th west to view several of the finest old homes in Anacortes, ending at H Avenue at the house built for the city's namesake, Anna Curtis Bowman, in 1891. Here you can walk down toward the water, turning north along the channel, the Guemes Island Ferry and a small public beach. The walk north along the channel back to town is along old railroad tracks past abandoned canneries to one of the oldest structures in town, Curtis Wharf, where you can muse among the tumbled buildings and rotting piers. A log on the tiny beach adjacent looking past old pilings across the channel to Guemes Island, strikes me as a great place for an urban picnic (you're only five blocks from Gere-a-Deli). From here you may want to amble along more quiet streets to look at houses, then back to your starting point downtown.

PARKS

Anacortes is remarkable for its parks. Early in the century several far-sighted citizens deeded some sizable blocks of land to the city, and these parks and forest lands make up much of the extensive green you see in and around the town. One of the interesting contrasts is the industrial impact, including massive clearcutting, seen against the ongoing preservation of certain environmental amenities.

A tour of Anacortes parks, for me, begins with **Washington Park**. Here you can drive, or preferably walk, the loop road around Fidalgo Head, moving from sandy beaches to tide pools to deep forest to rocky promontories showing a wide array of island ecology, all within the space of a brisk stroll. Add the camping facilities, boat launch, playground and picnic areas, and you have just about the complete park; it's one of my favorites, anywhere.

Another park worth searching out is **Little Cranberry Lake**. Part of the Community Forest Lands, the lake forms part of a wetlands area of beaver marshes and ponds, and is a good example of the region's wetland ecology, with an intricate system of trails to be explored. To circumambulate the lake is a pleasant way to spend a sunny afternoon.

Most of the **Anacortes Community Forest Lands**, in all 2,200 acres of public forest managed for preservation and recreational use, lie outside the city limits, near and around Mt. Erie to the south of town. Combined with state and regional parks and beach and lake access (there are 11 lakes on the island, most of them accessible), the Forest Lands provide a rich resource for outdoor recreation. If you want to hike these lands, a **Trail Guide** is available at bookstores and other places around town.

Back in the city, a good place to take the kids is **Storvik Park** with its award-winning playground sculpture as well as baseball field and basketball courts, and rolling lawns. And don't forget about the little beaches at the ends of certain streets around the peninsula. The city has published an **Access Guide** to all the beaches in the area available for public use. For detailed information about the beaches, parks and other recreational activities in Anacortes, call or stop by the city **Parks and Recreation Department**.

HISTORY & ART

Where the history of these smaller west coast towns has not been obliterated by urbanization, suburbanization or shopping malls, there is quite a rich, living record of the past, despite the fact that rarely does the evidence go back over a hundred years. Many smaller cities are reaping the benefit of increasing concern for historical preservation, and appear to have escaped the blight of growing too fast too soon. In Anacortes there is a fond regard and public support for the somewhat colorful memorabilia of the place, as shown in support for the museum, Old Depot restoration and other historical projects. Even where development occurs, as at Ship Harbor near the state ferry terminal, public concern has demanded preservation of a rare wetland and an interpretive center for traditional Indian culture, as part of the planned complex of shops, condos, and marina.

While Anacortes has not gone to the extreme of little plaques to date the buildings, there is a tour guide to the more notable historical structures, available at shops and at the **Chamber of Commerce** office. However, you can see most of the history of the place on your own, just by walking the business and residential streets. A visit to the **Anacortes Museum**, itself a historical structure (a former Carnegie Library) located in an area of certain historical interest, is a good way to get a feeling for the bygone eras of logging done by men and animals, fish processing by Chinese laborers, and the texture of the place when it was truly a frontier town.

And have you been noticing, as you explore the town, those life-size figures built as facia on certain buildings? Some of them look so real from a distance they seem almost to be real people all dressed up and leaning against a wall. A labor of love by a group of local artists, these "murals" are taken from old photos of Anacortes scenes and characters, placed in or near their original setting (the mechanic at the old gas station on Commercial; the flivver on the wall of the Chevy dealership) and bring some of the town's history very much alive.

The history of the place is alive, too, in the preservation of traditional wooden boatbuilding and in the restoration of classic craft. It's a pleasure to see the occasional well-preserved wooden sailing boat in the marinas, or a big wooden craft under construction at Freya Boat on 3rd. And at the end of July you can trek out to Bowman Bay at Deception Pass and see the local builders' fine wooden boats in the Old Anacortes Rowing Society annual Regatta.

The arts are as lively as history in Anacortes. The Skagit Valley and environs are noted for the artists who live here, and there are several top regional talents working on Fidalgo and Guemes Islands, as well as among the San Juans. The **Anacortes Art Gallery**, a community gallery run entirely by volunteers, displays work of the area's artists in monthly shows as well as ongoing exhibits of pottery, jewelry and the like. Just up the street, the **Green Frog Gallery** shows primarily the work of regional printmakers. And at the annual **Arts & Crafts Festival** artists in virtually all media from the entire Northwest participate in invitational and juried shows at the Depot.

In keeping with the excellent series of maps and guides to places of interest put out by various agencies and groups, the **Chamber of Commerce** has published a pamphlet called "Landmarks, Monuments & Art in Public Places," with photos and directions for seeing the many interesting art works around town. Two that are easy to see are at the Post Office: inside, a WPA mural by Kenneth Callahan depicting purse-seine fishermen; and out front is a small bronze bird family by famed Geumes Island artist Philip McCracken.

SHOPPING

A stroll up Commercial Ave through Old Anacortes will yield several shops that are unique to this town and which will provide some interesting browsing, as well as possibly something special to send home to the folks. Start with the **Marine Supply & Hardware** where eighty years of outfitting everybody from fishermen to farmers has left an astonishing array of unlikey implements and gizmos. If you're into boating you'll be especially happy snooping around this store.Walk a couple of blocks south to **Nineteenth Century Antiques**, in the same building as the Anacortes Art Gallery, where the combination of contemporary crafts and fine antiques and replicas makes for a rewarding visit. A couple of blocks more and you come to the Shannon Building, built in 1891, on the corner of 6th & Commercial. In this elegant restoration, **Friendly Books** displays a good selection of books about the Valley and the Islands, as well as standard bookstore fare. Sharing the front of the Shannon Building is **The Quotation**, a shop unlike anything I've seen anywhere, where hundreds of memorable (and goofy) quotes have been written out in calligraphy, printed, then hand colored, matted and framed. There's a quotation for just about anybody, an inexpensive and unusual souvenir.

In the next block south you come to another unusual store, **Potlatch Gifts**, operated by the Samish Indian Tribe. The store sells Indian arts and crafts in the Coast Salish style, including the famous hand-knit wool sweaters, custom made for each wearer. At Potlatch you can also see a model of the interpretive center planned by the tribe for the complex at Ship Harbor. One more block finds you at the corner where Old Town becomes not-so-old town, at the eclectic **Left Bank Antiques**, where many of the pieces are searched out by the owner, who has a good eye for the unexpected, in England.

ENTERTAINMENT

Anacortes doesn't offer much in the way of nightlife, at least not in the regular doses dwellers in larger cities have grown used to. There are no clubs where you can catch live jazz any night of the week, for instance. There are quite a few taverns. If that's your style, try **Maggie's Alibi** for burgers, beer and the bar sports. There are cocktail lounges at Slocum's and Boomer's Landing and at a couple of downtown restaurants. On Friday and Saturday nights you can dance to live music at the **Square Rigger**. Occasionally a singing or performing group appears somewhere in town, and you usually can find notice of it in the local newspaper, the Anacortes American, published on Wednesdays.

One excellent possibility is the **Anacortes Community Theatre**. An energetic and exacting amateur group, ACT presents at least four plays per year, so the house is seldom dark for long. The **Skagit Valley Symphony**, an emerging amateur orchestra, plays at least four performances in Anacortes during its season, usually at **Brodniak Hall** on the High School campus, a handsome, spacious hall considered to be technically one of the finest theatres in the Northwest. Also at Brodniak Hall, the **Anacortes Repertory of Theatres** presents a wide variety of professional companies in music, dance and drama, with at least one performance a month throughout the year.

You might be lucky enough to be in town for one of two annual performances that draw crowds hereabouts. The last weekend in July is scheduled for two performances, Friday and Saturday nights, of the barbershop singing group the AnoCords, at Brodniak Hall. At the same theater in December, the Vela Luka Dancers present music and dance of the local Croatian community.

If all else fails, and there's nothing you want to

see at the **Anacortes Cinema**, you can always go bowling.

INDOOR & OUTDOOR SPORTS

Seriously, the bowling alley, **San Juan Lanes**, is also a pizza parlor and burger joint, with a cocktail lounge on the side, and the next-door video palace, **Tubes**, is a kids' hangout. So if you can stand the noise, and the kids, and bowling, it's a surefire way to find something lively going on almost any night.

The other indoor sports activity that's very popular in Anacortes is swimming. **Fidalgo Pool** is a competition-grade pool used extensively by the schools and the community. You will also find a tanning room, sauna and high-tech exercise equipment for use at low fees. The pool is often filled with classes or groups, so it's a good idea to call or pick up a schedule before dropping in.

Tennis courts are near the **Anacortes Middle School**, and since they are school district courts, occasionally you might find them filled with students. There are outdoor basketball courts at **Storvik Park**, and on Tuesdays at noon you can find an open basketball game on the court in the basement of City Hall. Call or stop in at the **Parks & Recreation Department** for information on other sports programs that might be open to drop-ins.

For golf you have to drive a few miles out of town, on Highway 20 east , to the **Similk Beach Golf Course**, eighteen holes on a lovely stretch of lowland between Fidalgo Bay on the north and Similk Bay on the south.

BIG EVENTS

The major annual event in Anacortes is the **Arts & Crafts Festival**, held the first weekend of August. Over the years the Festival has grown from an art exhibit and street fair, to include the Anacortes Steam Railway, an antique car show and a broad range of cultural events. When the Depot was opened a couple of years ago, the festival spread physically from Commercial Avenue out along 7th Street, so that now most of the downtown is involved. The festival draws thousands during its two-day run, and also draws some of the best artists and craftsmen to the juried shows and street fair.

The weather around the first of August is almost always fine (no rain on the festival, they say, for over 20 years), so those weekends are usually set for the other big events in town: the **Old Anacortes Rowing Society** regatta; the Park & Recreation **Ride, Row, Run Relay**; and the **An-O-Cords** Barbershop Quartet Concert and Salmon Barbeque. And mid-August is the time for the World's Biggest King Salmon Barbeque, sponsored by the **Anacortes Eagles**. It's a good time to be visiting.

Weather is the impetus for other annual events around Anacortes. In April when the tulips, daffodils and iris bloom in the Valley, and winter is definitely over, Anacortes hosts the immensely popular **Taste of Skagit**, an eating festival featuring the fine restaurants from all around Skagit County and the Islands. During April, too, is the annual blessing of the fishing fleet, at Cap Sante Boat Haven, and a boat show, usually held at the National Guard Armory on M Avenue.

But speaking of weather, I never mentioned the

skies of Anacortes. It's surprisingly dry and mild most of the time, being in the rain shadow of the Olympics, tempered by the surrounding water. But storms do arrive, from the north out of the Straights of Georgia, and from the southeast, across Skagit Valley and up the Saratoga Passage. Because of all the water, the broad, clear, sloping peninsula, and the many vantage points, you see a lot of sky here. When the weather is changing, or the wind shifting, the battles between clouds and pressure fronts are visible for miles. I have mentioned the spectacular views; next time you're here, watch for spectacular skies.

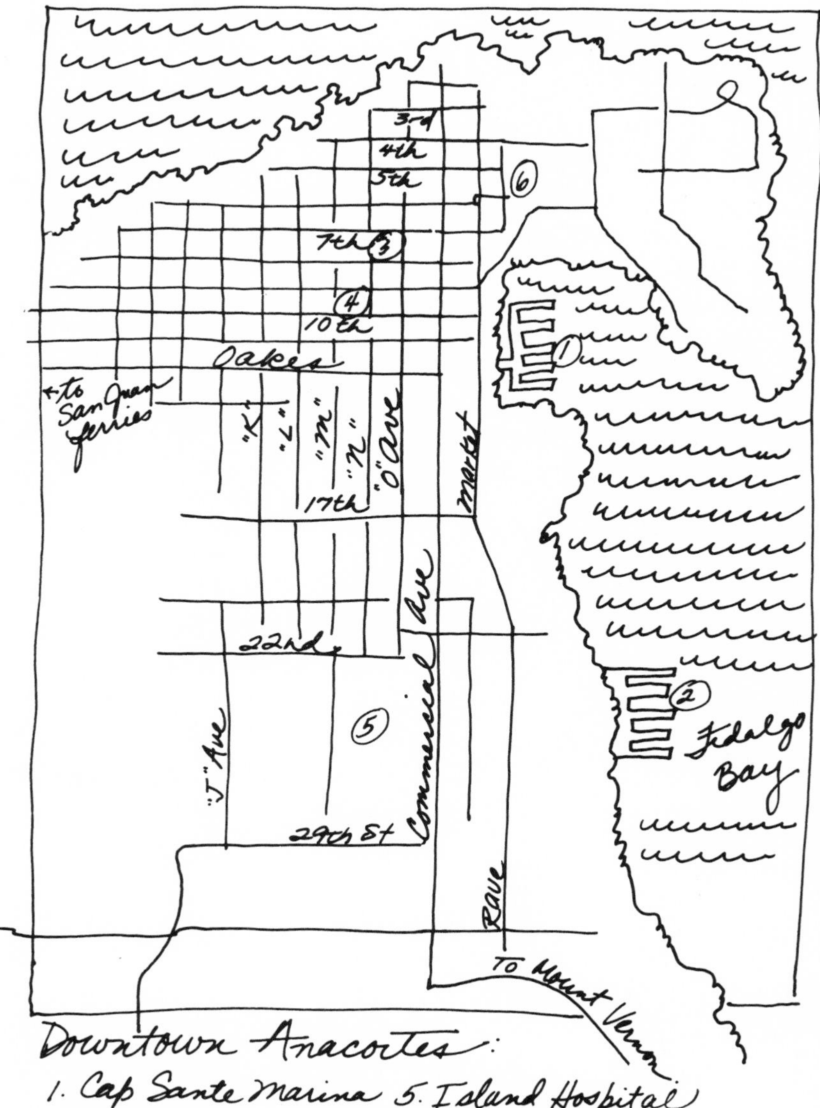

Downtown Anacortes:

1. Cap Sante Marina
2. Anacortes Marina
3. Causland Park
4. Library
5. Island Hospital
6. Old depot

Anacortes Index

Bellingham
by the Dock of the Bay

Even though it's always been considered one of the best harbors on the West Coast, Bellingham must have been a pretty lonely outpost through those years when what was going on was resource extraction and the people who lived here were sending all the product of their work away. When the value of the resources fell, Bellingham suffered and dwindled. But the place has such wealth of resources that there has always been a place for those people who have worked at pulling them out of the earth, off the earth, out of the sea.

Bellingham grew up a little late, as cities along the West Coast go. When Washington was becoming a state, and Seattle was boisterously rebuilding itself after its big fire, just at the time when the railroad was reaching to the ports on Puget Sound, Bellingham was still a cluster of four small towns dotted around the bay, each separated by dense forest. By 1900 the four towns had consolidated, Bellingham had been chosen as a site for one of the state normal schools (teacher's colleges: the others are at Ellensburg and Cheney near Spokane), and the city had a population of just over thirteen thousand.

That isn't to say that the towns of Whatcom, New Whatcom, Sehome and Fairhaven didn't have their day. Demands for resources boomed at various times all through the history of the place, and real estate speculation and gold rush fever, too. At different times the size and wealth of these communities beside the bay swelled, and there has always been some pretty solid wealth coming out of those mines, forests and waters, as is evidenced by the many grand homes, especially around Sehome Hill. The boom of the early 1890s, fired by the expectation so many towns had of being a major rail terminus, virtually built the town of Fairhaven-- and when the railway went to Seattle and the panic of the later 90s struck, Fairhaven was hit so hard some of the buildings were never finished.

Boom and bust and growing up late are not uncommon to cities along the Sound, and most of them show remnants of days of greater glory. Bellingham really began to take on the economic zip and the frazzled edges of a modern city with the coming of the Interstate Freeway in the early 1960s and the concurrent burst in the size of the college, as the war babies began to come of age. I was one of the early war babies at Western and not even the two-lane highway prevented me and my confreres from taking off whenever possible for weekends in Vancouver, Seattle and even San Francisco a time or two. We thought we were that far out on the edge of things.

But the place has always had a tough, intelligent, mellow heart. When the old city hall, which had become a museum, suffered a fire in 1962, the community rallied to rebuild it. It was an early and impressive inner city restoration project that is now visually one of the most striking elements of Bellingham and one of the finest museums in the state. And it was the hip war-baby generation that saved Old Fairhaven, by being interested in it, and using it, during the period of the rush to the shopping malls. So Bellingham has preserved much of the exuberance and optimism of its past. Where the harsh realities, such as the downtown pulp mill, obtrude, well, it is the dock of the bay, after all.

ARRIVALS

If you reach Bellingham from the south via Interstate 5, by the time you've gotten through the Chuckanut Mountains south of town the freeway has become grueling and the driving dogged. You can plow on determinedly, maybe stopping at a Motel Six and continue to face that bleak concrete strip into the northern wilderness all the way to Alaska, and never see Bellingham. What you see is what you see on the freeway edges of most cities, and to see Bellingham you have to take any downtown exit and keep going west until you actually get downtown. The same applies coming from the north, perhaps without the doggedness. The Lakeway exit is the most direct to downtown, with a minimum number of freeway excressences, and it puts you at the top of Holly St, a major one-way street into the city center that lets you have a fairly good overlook of the place as you arrive.

If you arrive by public transportation, you'll find that the **Greyhound Bus Depot** is a classic of the form. Now much reduced in function, this facility once represented, at least in my mind, perfect urban Americana, right down to the ticket and baggage windows, the lunch counter (now long gone) and the phone booths. And for your short Bellingham adventure, the bus sets you down just a hop from city bus lines and the heart of town. Before you take off, walk around the corner and have a look at the building. If I were going to restore the rest of Bellingham I'd finish Fairhaven, then start here.

Arrivals by air land at **Bellingham International Airport**, several miles to the northwest via I-5. Service to and from major nearby cities is provided by **PSA** and by **San Juan Airlines**. Rental car service is available at the airport; many of the larger motels offer courtesy car service; taxicabs, such as **Allknight** or **Superior** charge about $9 for a trip between the airport and downtown.

Sports mariners will dock at the city marina in **Squalicum Harbor**, a large and well-serviced facility welcoming moorages of all sizes. A taxi ride to the city center costs about $4, the number 10B bus serves the harbor, and it's not an unpleasant walk.

PLACES TO STAY

Bellingham needs the **Leopold Hotel**. The Leopold was the last of Bellingham's major downtown hotels, now refurbished and in use as a residential hotel for retired persons. While not as significant architecturally as the grand hotels in some cities, nevertheless the Leopold had all the trappings-- snazzy lobby, gift shop, ballroom-- and that connection with the street that was destroyed by the auto and the motel. Much of the original grandeur of the lobby has been uncovered, and you can at least get inside and have a look at the big chandelier. And the restored Crystal Ballroom is available for rent, so if you're with a group or convention you might consider it as a special place to meet. (I have actually crooned out saxophone tunes in that ballroom as a music student at Western.)

So, if you can't tip the doorman at the Leopold, the next closest thing to a downtown hostelry is the **Travelodge Motel**, right at one of the busiest streetcorners in the city. There you can put the car away and get out on the streets and look around.

The rest of the motels are just motels; many of them are found along Samish Way and close to I-5. Most of the big chains are represented. If you want to stay at a place with some trees around, try the **Evergreen Motel** on the way out to Lake Padden and the golf course.

However, for accomodations that are a little more expressive of the place you're visiting, you might try the ever-blossoming bed & breakfast scene which is as popular in Bellingham as it is elsewhere in the Northwest. For example, the ten-room **North Garden Inn** is tucked on the side of Sehome Hill midway between the town and the university in one of those lovely big frame homes with a view of the bay from some rooms. Another, **Heron Reach**, is within a short walk of the Fairhaven District and Fairhaven Park. Another overnight experience in the granduer of yesteryear might be found at **The Castle**, one of Fairhaven's finest houses. Some B & Bs are in fine older homes, some have views, some are near parks or points of interest. Most of them have two or three rooms available. The best way to get a line on the vagueries of this hostelry is to call **BaB's Reservation Service**. Let them know what your interests and requirements are and see what they come up with.

Campers are in luck. Just to the south of town, on Chuckanut Drive, is **Larrabee State Park**, for tents and RVs, with access to the bay and plenty of woods and trails for a idyllic stay.

GETTING AROUND

Distances are a little too great to walk comfortably from place to place except around the very center of town. The university is a long uphill climb (if you're no longer a student), and Fairhaven is serious hiking distance. The harbor is pushing the limit for a lot of people. But each of these outlying destinations is complex enough to warrant getting out of the car and walking around, and they are all on direct transit routes. The bus system here is a good one, and the **Transit Terminal** provides a central focus for getting around by bus, as well as a place to get in out of the rain. (Did you notice the stained glass work above the doors?) Have a look at the transit map there (it's also in the phone book) to see how you could organize a sightseeing tour on two or three bus routes.

SEEING THE SIGHTS

Better to take looking at Bellingham in several pieces, since the things to see are in clusters, separated from one another by some distance.

A downtown walk is most satisfying just meandering the rather shapely streets. I mean, the streets are not just grids, and the conjuntion of the several cities and the curve of the bay have left some shape to the downtown infrastructure, so you get nice triangles, unusual curves. Using State Street as your boundary on the southeast, and Whatcom Creek on the northeast, try weaving the streets between Holly and, say, Cornwall, heading generally northwest till you come to the **Whatcom Museum**. That is downtown Bellingham, much of it unchanged for decades. Your overlook from the museum is of industrial/port/waterfront Bellingham and what has always been called Old Town, the route of your next walk.

If you start at Holly and Railroad and walk toward the water, then walk along the water and back to Holly, then continue along the bay on Holly, you will get a taste of industrial/maritime Bellingham. Also along Holly you will find the old buildings and antique shops and cafes of the old part of town, when I was a student haunts for cheap meals and cheap clothes. If you're ambitious you can walk as far as the marina at Squalicum Harbor to see the activities of working boatyards, marine chandlers and so on. If you make a slight detour (two blocks up) you can have a look at the **George Pickett House**, built in the late 1850s. Pickett, who came here as a captain to help quell Indian uneasiness, later led the Confederate charge at Gettysburg. Stories of his exploits here and on San

Juan Island, and of his scout Blanket Bill Jarman, crop up frequently in regional histories.

A walk at **Western Washington University** requires transportation to get there; buses 3, 5 and 8 serve the campus. Start at Old Main, the original college building, renovated and kept alive as the heart of the institution, and either take the guided tours or wander off on your own. It's a beautiful campus most any time of year. The architecture is varied and some of it unusual, and the outdoor sculpture collection is a major achievement. If you're on your own be sure to ask at Old Main for the printed catalog of the collection so you can find it all. There are several spectacular outlooks from various places around the campus; for an even finer view, drive around the south campus to College Parkway and up Sehome Hill to the arboretum and overlook there.

A visit to **Old Fairhaven** is a concentrated tour of turn-of-the-century architecture reminiscent of Pioneer Square in Seattle, only reduced in scale so that every structure stands out, and you can get a picture of what the exuberance of the early 1890's must have been like. But there's a great deal more than just architecture here. Fairhaven has been going through a long revival and has developed into a true community almost as distinct from the rest of Bellingham as it was in the days of the four seperate towns. Within an area of eight or ten square blocks you can see the several notable buildings and poke into the shops, restaurants, bookstores and the coffeehouse. You get a sense of good fellowship that prevails here, and the commitment folks have about preserving and enhancing the physical and social attractiveness of the place. Among the places of note are the Mason Block of 1889, now called the Marketplace, probably the most extensive restoration in the district; the Carnegie-financed **Fairhaven Library** of 1904, still in continuous use; and the several antique railway cars which provide a nice contrast to the brick and stone structures, and augment the history of the place. For a longer walk, trek on out Chuckanut Drive to the south for a look at the beautifully restored house right at the beginning of the drive, and, farther on, Fairhaven Park with its formal rose garden.

PLACES TO EAT

Since you're in Old Fairhaven, here's a sampling of the several eateries in the district. A couple of them are worth coming back to for a serious dinner, for example, **The Fairhaven Restaurant**, presents an ambitious dinner menu, mostly of seafood, along with an extensive wine list including local (Mt. Baker Winery) and regional labels. It's a very popular place, and a good lunch or dinner focus for a visit to the district. Of the many Mexican restaurants in Bellingham, **Dos Padres** is one of the notables, serving traditional fare along with some rather unusual dishes. You can get a hefty breakfast here at 6:30, and there's a lounge, usually with some kind of live music in the background.

One of my favorite spots in Old Fairhaven is **Tony's Coffees & Teas**, where you can stop for an espresso or cappucino and pastries anytime during the day or evening, and in the evening there's live entertainment, too. I also like the intermixing of cafe and bookstore at **The Colophon Cafe** next door to Village Books. The combination creates a stimulating atmosphere appropriate to a college town.

EATING IN DOWNTOWN BELLINGHAM

In any university town the number of places to eat is higher than elsewhere, especially places that serve burgers, sandwiches and pizza. In Bellingham there are a surprising number of fine restaurants as well, and places serving seafood and ethnic cooking.

For a restaurant with a view, and a solid menu of steaks and seafood, **The Cliff House** offers a view of Bellingham Bay unsurpassed by any other dinner establishment in town. Another view restaurant worth knowing about is **High Country** in the Bellingham Tower. If fine dining is your sport, then you should definitely plan a dinner at **M'sieur's**. Housed in a nicely converted gas station, this restaurant has won a high reputation regionally for its treatment of seasonal seafood and meats from local growers. Italian cuisine is well represented, in a decorative atmosphere that helps make for a real night out, at **Il Fiasco**, with its carefully-done pasta dishes and provincial cooking.

Seafood ought to be among the best here by the bay, and if you want to try it out, plan dinner at the **Bristol Bay Fish Co.** where they concentrate on preparing dishes from Puget Sound waters. I've always liked those restaurants located right on the docks amongst the working boats, where you can feel as though the salmon is still wriggling when it hits the saute. Such a place is **Harbor House** in the Marina.

Of the number of Chinese restaurants in Bellingham, one of my favorites is the **Oriental Star**, a small place that serves variations on European and

Oriental cooking. While it's not right in the heart of things, its reputation deserves a trip to **Uncle Chen's** for excellent Szechuan cuisine. In another mode, the rather hip, organic style of **The Oasis** is attractive (and delicious), especially for its lunches and homemade desserts.

I'm going to clear out the cars from Railroad Ave, plant a few trees there and run an old trolley along the tracks, then go sit mornings at **The Bagelry** where the morning light in the big open space makes a nice place to sit over the news and good coffee and a chewy bagel. Over by the Mt. Baker Theatre is the **Pacific Cafe**, a very pretty spot where there is a serious pastry chef in residence. Serious breakfast eaters will want to know about the home-style cooking at the **Old Town Cafe**. This is the site of the former Matt & Millie's from my college days, and the nostalgia alone makes it worth a visit, not to mention the hashbrowns and the counterculture types hanging out just like old times. Farther along toward the marina, in the Fisherman's Market, is the **Shrimp Shack**, which I would call a perfect example of the Northwest Washington cafe, long the place for take-out deep-fry seafood, chowder, shrimp cocktails and the like-- kind of an Ivar's Old Town style.

Out on a date? Kids giving you a hard time? Take 'em to **Bunk's**. It's a real drive-in, with *carhops* . Some things never change.

Finally, a couple of things you might want to keep in mind: there is an espresso wagon that hangs out in front of the Post Office, corner of Cornwall and Magnolia, in case you need refreshment on your downtown walk; and just down Cornwall there is a classic Woolworth's, complete with lunch counter and soda fountain, maybe the last one left in the state.

PARKS

You never quite get away from the natural setting of Bellingham, and despite the industrial monoliths on the harbor, there is always the sense that the forest could creep right back down to the water the way it was when Roeder and Co set up the first sawmill and began whittling away at it. They've been hauling out old second growth around here for years, scraping away at Chuckanut, but in some of the parks you can drop out of the urban environment and feel the forest creeping back.

At **Whatcom Falls Park** you will find Whatcom Creek cascading through stands of forest, with trails for walking and losing yourself in the setting. It's interesting to note that it was here that the first sawmill was established; now it's back to forest. The adjacent **Bloedel-Donavan Park** allows access to the northwest corner of Lake Whatcom, with a swimming area and a public boat launch. City bus number 4 reaches both these parks.

Bellingham's formal park is **Cornwall Park** which differs from the formal parks in many cities in that rather than presenting traditional vistas and tidy plantings, Cornwall Park is dominated by trees, giving it a quiet coolness, especially in the summer-- it's a wonderful picnic spot. Take city bus number 9 to reach Cornwall Park.

To combine forest walks with a spectacular view of the city, the bay, and the San Juans beyond, take a trek to the top of **Sehome Hill Park & Arboretum**. It's kind of a long walk from the bus stop (numbers 5 and 8), but you can drive right up to the viewpoint and start your walk from there. If you're interested in trees, there are some beautiful and varied and unusual specimens here. Finally, for woods and natural settings, the extensive **Lake Padden Park** at the head of Padden Creek, is some distance from the heart of town, but you can reach it via bus number 5, and you'll find enough space and activities to while a lot of time. The public golf course is also located out here.

Padden Creek also runs through one of the nicest parks in the area, the formal **Fairhaven Park** at the beginning of Chuckanut Drive in Fairhaven. Here the attractions are the flower beds and rock gardens, and the rose garden, which is a significant collection.

Parks also grace the shoreline. **Marine Park** is a short walk from the Fairhaven District and helps to complete a view of the connection this city once had with the sea. Along State Street between Fairhaven and downtown Bellingham, **Boulevard Park** is a sizeable stretch of shoreline ideal for picnics and poking along the water's edge. City Bus number 1 takes you close to the parks around the Fairhaven District.And the jewel, if somewhat rough, in this crown of parks is **Maritime Heritage Park**. It's one of the most intriguing urban parks I've seen. At the mouth of Whatcom Creek, where it tumbles into a small estuary, there is a salmon hatchery and fish ladder, with walks and views and stretches of lawn. You can explore here for hours.

Finally, keep an eye out, as you walk Bellingham streets, for places where Whatcom Creek snakes under an old bridge, with maybe a scrap of lawn and a bench or two along its banks. These tiny pocket parks can make a summer stroll a real pleasure.

HISTORY AND ART

Bellingham has done as well as any city in the Northwest at rediscovering and preserving its heritage wherever possible, and the **Whatcom County Museum of History & Art** is an excellent example of the dedication and cohesive vision this community has shown toward its cultural artifacts. The building itself is an excellent example. Built as an extravagant city hall in 1892 to welcome the hoped-for coming of the railroad, the building had already been put into use as a museum when it was seriously burned in 1962. The building seemed lost, but through much community effort was restored and is now not only one of the city's major visual elements, but is one of the top museums in the region as well. The collections of Northwest Indian Art, pioneer logging and fishing implements, and superb Darius Kinsey photographs, among others, are complemented by changing exhibits of contemporary Northwest art in an innovative and very classy program.

Several other buildings containing memorabilia from Whatcom's early days are open for visits and tours. The **George Pickett House**, built between 1856 and 1860 by the famous military leader, is maintained by the Washington State Historical Society and contains a collection of objects from the very early days of the settlement. Another very old structure you can visit is the old **County Court House**, built in 1858, which has seen many uses over the years. The **Roeder Home**, built in 1908, is now used as a cultural center for art exhibits and classes and music performances. While you're exploring, keep your eyes open for the many unusual buildings that mark various periods in the city's history, such as the Mt. Baker Theatre, the Bellingham Herald Building (and several others along that stretch of State Street) and the unusual Bon Marche.

A tour of the historic buildings can be enhanced by a look at the contemporary art that is shown at several of the galleries in the downtown part of Bellingham. In Old Town, amongst the antiques and industrial remnants you'll find **The Elements Gallery** that pursues a program of showing local artists, and nearby the **Matter-Danz Gallery**, agents and exhibitors for regional work in several media. Another project in Old Town housing several shops and businesses is Bay Street Village, where you'll find the **Blue Horse Gallery** in an unusual and effective exhibit space, with a large selection of prints.

Mention has already been made of the living history you'll find in the buildings of Fairhaven; living art can also been seen, and purchased, at **Gallery West**. Also mentioned was the outdoor sculpture museum at Western. You might want to have a look at the Art Department's second floor gallery as well.

SHOPPING

While downtown Bellingham has a somewhat condensed version of the zone of major department, clothing and shoe stores and boutiques that you find in major cities-- it has a Bon Marche, for example, in an unusual building-- there are several complexes of shops that are unique to Bellingham, and show off some of the nice old buildings to good advantage. Right near the center of town you'll find the **Bellingham Hardware**

Building, a very well-done interior remodel of a handsome and well preserved older building. At **The Greenhouse** a store full of unusual and interesting objects combine with an unusual building to make for rewarding browsing, and a block further on, **Bay Street Village**, also mentioned for the gallery it contains: a handy combination of browsing all within a few blocks-- architecture, art, and just plain stuff.

Antiques abound, especially along W Holly in Old Town. For a building chock-full of antiques visit the **Bellingham Antique Mall,** where you can get a close look at the objects that once adorned the old homes and business establishments of this city in a graceful building that's the centerpiece of the downtown stores. For rare books and books about antiques and collecting **Bristol Antiques** can give knowledgeable help.

One of the first places I went when I began researching this book was **Village Books** in Old Fairhaven, where there is an excellent section of Northwestiana. One bookstore wall opens onto the Colophon Cafe, so it's an easy matter to combine two of my favorite hobbies.

A NIGHT ON THE TOWN

We always used to say there wasn't much to do in Bellingham, but a quick glance at various calendars shows that isn't true. All you need to do is check out the schedule at the **WWU Performing Arts Center**, and you'll probably find something going on some night that during your visit. The **Bellingham Symphony**, a top-rate orchestra composed of members of the WWU music faculty as well as community musicians, performs here, as does the **Whatcom Community Chorale** and the **Whatcom Youth Orchestra**. That's not to mention performances by various musical and dramatic organizations at the University, and presentations by visiting performers of all kinds. For instant information on what might be happening at the Center, when you visit the campus check the reader board in front of the Library, or pick up a copy of the campus newspaper.

Two other places in the community that schedule regular musical presentations are the **Whatcom Museum** and the **Roeder Home**. The museum offers a wide range of programs including films and lectures.

Bellingham has a long-standing drama troupe, the **Bellingham Theatre Guild** that has achieved a high reputation. The company has its own theatre, kind of a landmark here for years, and presents several plays during its season. Another stage to know about is the **Old Main Theatre**, which usually presents student actors and directors in this intimate little theatre setting.

If you're looking for dinnertime or nightclub-style entertainment, there's a whole potpourri of possibilities for casual drop-in entertainment at Old Fairhaven, from the solo guitar usually playing at Dos Padres or the offerings at The Fairhaven or Tony's, to the lounge attractions at **Venus Pizza**, where there seems to be enough going on, what with the big TV screen and the music and the pizza, to keep you occupied all evening, if that's your style.

In downtown Bellingham much the same applies. In the old days many of us liked the scene at **The Royal Lounge** with its piano bar and so on, and scene is much the same. Now the Royal hosts "battles of the bands" some weekend nights, so the sounds can get pretty raucous. A variety of different events happen, and different performing groups appear, at the Ballroom of **Holiday Inn**, so you might want to cruise out there and check the reader board.

Another place to watch, for events besides the movies, is the **Mount Baker Theatre**, one of the historic buildings you see on your downtown tour. They had the Peking Acrobats playing there when I was in town once. And don't forget the classic and foreign film fare at the **Fairhaven Cinema**.

INDOOR & OUTDOOR SPORTS

The readiest access to sports indoors in Bellingham are the Ys. The public indoor swimming pool is at the **YMCA**, along with a basketball court for pickup games and weight training gear among other things. The **YWCA** has an extensive recreation program, and you should call to see about accomodations for dropins.

There's always a good chance of catching a spectator sport at the University, whether in the spectacular gymnasium or in the playing fields to the south, and Bellingham's **Civic Field** hosts track and football and rugby meets. They play rugby here.

The region around Bellingham and Whatcom County is a heaven for the outdoor recreationist. From sailing on the bay and in the San Juans to skiing or hiking nearby Mt. Baker and the North Cascades, the city offers access to pretty much any outdoor sport the visitor can propose. Horseshoes? The pits at Cornwall Park are frequented by the addicts of that sport. Ready access to tennis courts is found at Fairhaven Park and at Lake Padden, which is also the nearest public golf course. There is a pleasant swimming beach at Bloedel-

Donovan Park as well as a boat launch. Boat launches onto the bay are at **Marine Park** and at **Squalicum Harbor**.

If you want to get out on the sound several yacht charter and boat rental places are available at or near the Marina. For sailing and/or fishing charters check with **San Juan Sailing**. The chandlery **Eddystone Light** is an outfitter for boaters, sells inflatable craft and stocks charts and sailing periodicals. Charters for sport fishing and whale watching can be arranged through **Wildlife Cruises**. Another popular water sport is river-rafting, in this case on the nearby Nooksack. Float trips are organized by **Huck Finn River Adventures**.

For trips into the mountains some of the best help and advice (and spiffy equipment) come from the outfitters, of which there are several in Bellingham. Hunting and fishing enthusiasts will want to check out **H & H Sporting Goods**; and for mountaineering of all kinds in all seasons, from skiing and crosscountry to backpacking and climbing, **Alpine West** offers rentals, maps, tips, etc., as does **Franz Gabl Sports Specialists**, where you can also arrange for kayaks and canoes. Touring the city on a bike on a nice day is pleasant and appropriate in this college town. **Fairhaven Bicycle** rents bikes.

BIG EVENTS

In fact, one of the most popular annual events in Bellingham, Fairhaven and Whatcom County is an extravaganza outdoor sporting event, the **Ski to Sea Relay**, held the last Sunday in May. The Ski-to-Sea is a weeklong community celebration of spring, centering on the race, which comprises six events and covers an 85-mile course, begins on

Mt Baker and ends up in the harbor at Fairhaven with a big party. Beginning with crosscountry skiing, the race moves through downhill skiing, a grueling downhill run, and bicycling. At this point the baton is passed to canoeists on the Nooksack who in turn pass on to sailors in various craft on Bellingham Bay. The race is a 1973 revival of a tradition going back to the Mt Baker Marathon of 1911-13, which was begun to help win a National Park for the area. Now the community rallies to celebrate the precious natural environment of these waters and mountains, and this city.

Other big annual events include the **Lummi Stommish Water Festival** at Goosebury Point on the nearby Lummi Indian Reservation at the end of June. Here is an opportunity to meet these splendid people and witness some of their celebritory events, including canoe racing. It's also an opportunity to take the ferry "Whatcom Chief" to Lummi Island.

In early August the summer art festival **Phantasmagoria** is held on the streets around the library and the courthouse. This is followed by the **Maritime Festival** later in the month, and the **Northwest International Art Competition** at the museum between late September and early November. Christmastime brings a series of weekend crafts shows in Fairhaven and a lighted boat parade in Bellingham Bay. For specific dates of these events you can get a current calendar from the **Visitor & Convention Bureau**.

Did I say Bellingham grows on you? I lived there a quarter of a century ago, just about, and in some ways it hasn't changed a bit. The bleak winds out of the Strait of Georgia are no less wet and cold now than then. In other ways it has become ever more liveable as its beauties become more appreciated and better expressed. And all along I've kept saying, I wouldn't mind living there again.

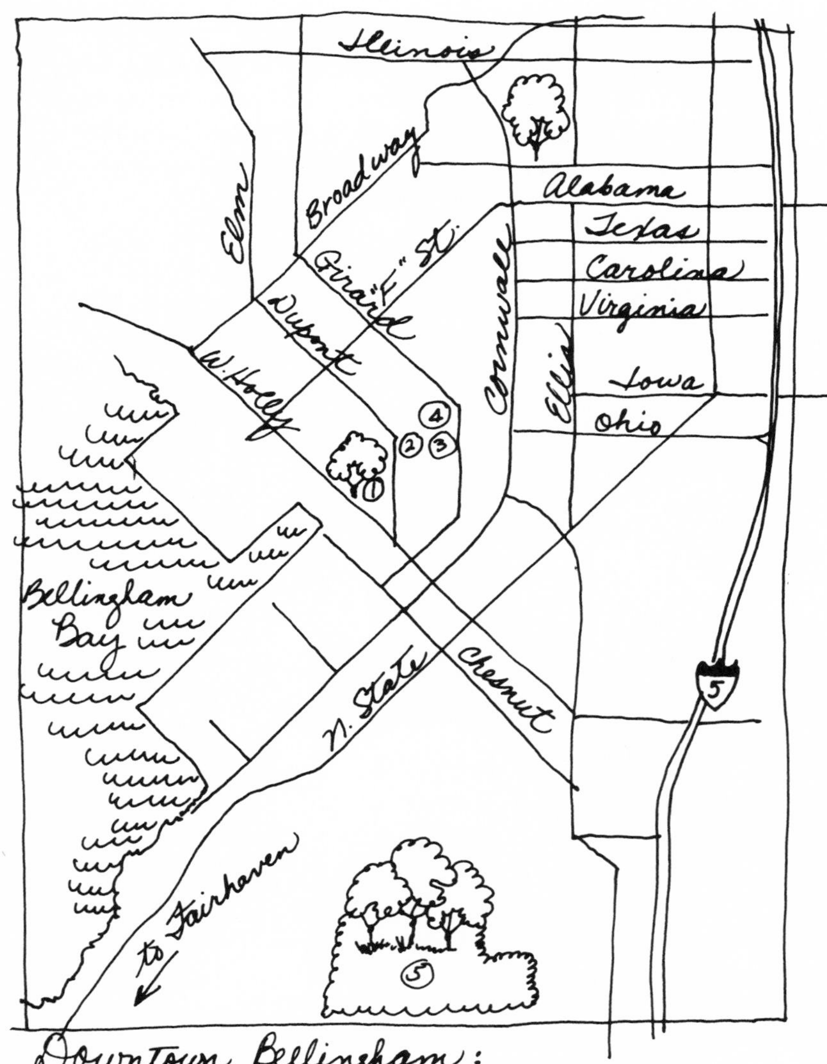

Downtown Bellingham:

1. Whatcom Co. Museum
2. Courthouse
3. Library
4. City Hall
5. Sehome Arboretum
6. Broadway Park

Bellingham Index

Wenatchee

Appleland

The river valleys of the east side drop abruptly out of the Cascades where their waters meet the Columbia as it loops close to the mountains in its mighty sweep across Washington to the south. The Methow, the Entiat and the Wenatchee drop between fingers of mountains, and at Lake Chelan you can see water locked up by those mountain reaches in a 60-mile-long cleft. Across the Columbia east lie the sere brown hills of North Central Washington; along the river valleys you can see the product of over a century of water reclamation-- the myriad and often tiny orchards clinging to any scrap of arable land that can be reached by irrigation.

With over three hundred days of sun, and the crisp cold days, just the right altitude (where it doesn't frost too late in the spring), this country, under irrigation, is just right for fruit trees. As one early orchardist put it, you can grow apple trees in sand if you can get water to them. So what you see when you arrive in this valley is the very productive use of water.

The early days were drier. Cattle-ranching was one of the first industries brought by settlers; several small gold strikes and the search for other minerals brought prospecters in advance of the sternwheeler riverboats pushing up the Columbia. But the first orchards were planted in the 1850s, and while the mines and the cattle ranches are still much in evidence, apple growing is obviously the thing that goes on here.

In Wenatchee the bountiful result of irrigation is seen at its best, and the growing of apples-- and other tree fruit but mostly apples-- gives the city an aspect of industry, especially during the harvest. Being situated at the crossroads of two major trans-state highways creates a bustle in the town that sometimes approaches the frantic, especially during vacation time. Wenatchee is a natural stopping place for travelers from the several directions, and there is a concentration of motels and fast food eateries that gives part of the town the aspect of an overnight stay. Travelers heading for the nearby resort areas of Lake Chelan and Mission Ridge also give the town a quality of a place one passes through. But at the same time orchards are a calm and patient sort of environment, and to take an afternoon or an extra day to get out of the car and have a look at the place will repay the visitor with some unusual views, excellent meals, quiet walks and interesting things to do.

ARRIVALS

Traveling from the west side across Stevens Pass (Highway 2) you follow the Wenatchee River from it source in the Cascades as it plummets into the Columbia. You also follow the once tortuous route of the Great Northern Railroad (about which more later). The apple orchards you begin to see as the pines thin out produce apples headed for the storage warehouses of Wenatchee, and it's fascinating to watch the changing terrain ans th increasing complexity of the orchard country as conditions and growing space coincide. Glimpses of the river and in some places its famous white water enhance the excitement of the vistas of dry country that open up as you descend into the valley.

The fast trip from the west side is via Interstate 90 across Snoqualmie Pass, then north through the Wenatchee Mountains along Highway 97 from Ellensburg. You pick up the Wenatchee River west of the city for a good view of the valley, and you also get some sense of just how rugged travel along the edges of the Cascades was for the early settlers.

From the north, approaching Wenatchee along Highway 97 as it follows the Columbia, the drop out of dry mountain foothills into the green of the valley is abrupt. You've just climbed over the brow of mountains separating the Wenatchee from the Entiat (in the old days folks had to cross the river twice to make that trip). South of the mammoth **Rocky Reach Dam** Highway 97 connects with Highway 2 from the west just at the river mouth, just at the city limits. The view to the east shows the rolling brown hills of the Basin framing the river and the valley as you drive into town. But soon you are distracted by the busy drive along the city streets that form the continuation of Highway 2 to Highway 28 toward Quincy and Euphrata right through the center of Wenatchee.

If you arrive from the east you have spent a goodly time in the vast reaches of the Coluimbia Basin, watching the Cascades, in glimpses, loom closer. Suddenly there is the river, and then there is that green valley.

Besides the many highway routes, Wenatchee is served by all forms of transportation. The municipal airport, **Pangborn Field**, is on the regular schedules of two regional airlines, **Cascade Airways** and **Horizon Air**. You can get to and from the airport for about $10 one way as far as the Convention Center downtown. The **Greyhound Bus Depot** is right downtown, about three blocks from the Convention Center. There is no public transit system in Wenatchee.

GETTING AROUND

Many city centers seem abandoned by the traffic due to freeways that skirt or are walled off from the center of town. Wenatchee has the opposite problem-- one that is both good and bad. A spur of Highway 2 runs right through the center of Wenatchee, crossing the river to connect with Highway 28 to the east. The traffic lends a sense of activity to the downtown streets, but at the cost of a steady flow of cars and trucks. That tends to intimidate anyone trying to rubberneck through a leisurely visit. Several parallel streets run north and south along the length of town above the river, while the east/west streets tend to be rather steep and to become residential within a few blocks. I found myself cruising these long one-way corridors in a kind of desperation just after I'd arrived, passing the same motels until I finally got oriented.

One approach I suggest is to turn off Wenatchee Avenue onto Mission or Chelan via one of the cross streets. Park on the shady side of the street (if you arrive in hot weather) and pause for awhile to check out your possibilities for lodging or eats. Getting lost can easily find you back on the highway out of town, so it's a good idea to become oriented with the map and the one-way streets before you set out again on your jaunts of discovery.

PLACES TO STAY

With the opening of the Best Western Motel at **Westerburg Plaza** just a block from the Convention Center, available accommodations have expanded beyond the many seemingly unvaried places along N. Wenatchee Avenue. This classy downtown motel complements the Convention Center, and between them they make a real step toward revitalizing the inner city. While you looking over the Westerburg Plaza, take alook across the street at the Cascadian, Wenatchee's grand hotel before it closed some years ago and was rebuilt as urban apartments. The Westerburg Plaza seems to update a tradition, and I enjoy the contrast in period architecture between the two buildings. For something a little less grand than the Westerburg, without the views of the river and the restaurant on the roof, but still in the very heart of Wenatchee, the **Uptowner Motel** is a short walk from the Greyhound Depot. It has a pool and a sauna and is close to government buildings, the museum, convention center and a couple of fine restaurants.

Along N. Wenatchee Avenue (where most of the motels are), there are two big hostelries that attract the convention crowds and are pretty busy all the time. The **Chieftan** is recommended by a lot of travelers. Since its restaurant is a popular hangout for locals, it's a pretty rollicking place. The **Thunderbird Motor Inn** seemed a little *too* crowded the last time i was in town, although there were vacancies, and I passed it up for a quieter place. You have to either mingle with the conventioneers or avoid them; they can't be ignored.

If you can get the right sort of room, away from the street and overlooking the Columbia, the **Orchard Inn**, a rather new motel done simply but in pretty good taste, can be aquiet place despite its proximity to a busy intersection. **Burgerbeers** is small, casual and inexpensive, with a comfortable restaurant attached. **Scotty's Motel** caters especially to skiers and charges reasonable rates. The proprietors are eager to provide advice on all sorts of activities in the out of doors.

Campers and RV travelers will find hookups and campsites nearby at **Lincoln Rock State Park** and at **Squilchuck State Park**.

EATING OUT

Wenatchee is even better supplied with restaurants than it is with motels, and for the same reason-- lots of people passing through. The fare runs the complete menu from famous steaks and gourmet ratings to the usual fast food reruns. Here on the edge of range country, the stomach turns to thoughts of steak and prime rib. If you want to experience an excellent steakhouse in the great tradition, include **The Windmill** in your plans for dining. It's small and very popular, so you should make reservations. For another approach to steak you might try the down home country and western style of **Murphy's** or the private booths and steak a la Black Angus at **Covey's**. Both these places also present live entertainment most nights.

The mansion fixed up as a restaurant here is **Horan House**. The extravagant structure was built by an early apple and water baron down by the river on the north side of town. The culinary style is eclectic with an emphasis on regional fare, and the atmosphere is of local history, with much of the original contents of the house left intact.

Seafood, due to some judicious importing by local restaurateurs, is as popular here as on the coast. The **Second Story**, a short walk from the Convention Center in the restored and converted **Morris Hardware Building** serves fresh seafood in the fine style with grace. **Steven's** in Mission Square specializes in the new "Northwest" cuisine, predictably with much seasonal seafood. As in other cities, these two restaurants demonstrate the concern for the renovation of traditional buildings along with the upbeat spirit that is so vital to the health of a resurging city center.

Checking out cuisines from other lands, two Mexican restaurants are worthy of note: the **Dos Rios Broiler** (try the chile rellenos) and, over across the river in East Wenatchee, **La Cocina**, for the emerging gourmet Mexican style. Family dining at **The Chieftan** could be quite an experience, all the way from the famous prime rib to the gregarious atmosphere. It's fun to find those cafes in any city, where the local folks and visitors mix it up. And it's open early (6 am) for breakfast, too. Another local institution that the kids might like is **Gino's Pizza**, an authentic parlor from the pioneer days of American Pizza.

Early breakfasts and all night joints are a little hard to find in Wenatchee. **Magnum's** is a fairly soft way to ease into the morning, with good coffee, but it opens a little late (7 am). The big **Four Seasons Inn** in East Wenatchee has an all-night coffee shop.

SEEING THE SIGHTS

Wenatchee is dominated by its remarkable setting, and, at all times of the year, by the incredibly intricate beauty of the apple orchards. To see views of the valley requires driving excursions on back roads up along the hills on both sides of the river, but I never tire of seeking out a new vantage point. The roads in and out of town offer some of the best viewpoints, as do the roads to **Mission Ridge** (south on Mission Street) and especially Methow Street, which you can pick up at Orondo near the county courthouse. Follow Methow south for spectacular rocky terrain outside the reaches of irrigation, past an old mine complete with tailings spilling to the roadside, to pick up Mission Street where it starts up the Squilchuck Valley toward the state park and Mission Ridge. You should consider a drive on up the valley to the Ridge if the weather is fine, for the broad vistas presented there. Returning to town along Mission the view reveals a band of rich river land (an intense green during growing season) set against the brown hills that mark the beginning of the great Columbia Basin.

A closer view of Wenatchee is made somewhat difficult by the vast apple storage and shipping complex along the railroad tracks above the river. But if you travel east on 5th past the Ice Arena, you'll come upon the recently completed **Riverfront Park**. It's a green strip of riverbank where you can walk and feel some of the town's relationship to the river, both as it is today and as it was in the days before the railroad and before the bridges, when sternwheelers docked nearby, pushing up the Columbia into new territory. To complete this quick look by car, drive back up 5th to **Wenatchee Valley College**, where you might want to take a look at the bulletin boards, as many of the performing arts events in the area take place here. Drive to Western Avenue and turn south for a tour through residential areas tucked up against dry hills. A circuitous route along Skyline Drive and Red Apple Road, past the swim and tennis club and the high school, leads to Miller Street where you turn left, arriving at **Triangle Park**, the **Apple Bowl**, and **Pioneer Park**. Traveling down Orondo returns you to the center of town.

A walking tour of Wenatchee (preferably done at times other than during the most severe heat or cold) might begin at the **Wenatchee Convention Center**, incorporate part of the downtown sector, the museum, the complex around the Chelan County Courthouse (built in 1924), and a glimpse of the restoration of older buildings going on around town. If you want to look at old buildings, the museum offers a sel-guided tour of the historic structures of Wenatchee. These walks will show you, for example, Mission Square and the **Liberty Theatre**, and I have mentioned the Morris Hardware Company building as an example among many of the kind of new spirit that can be engendered in a place when some loving attention is paid to its hidden beauties.

On another walk you could amble among the mammoth apple storage houses, which are massive sculptures in concrete and the random stacking of apple "totes" against them. If you wander along the tracks as Bridge Street, you can cross the Columbia on foot at **Pipeline Bridge** for a close view of the river and a returning picture of the city from an unusual vantage point. Hardier walkers might want to hike up Orondo past the courthouse, through a pleasant residential section, as far as Pioneer Park and Triangle Park and the Apple Bowl, focus of the annual eleven-day Apple Blossom Festival in the spring, the city's extravagant paean to the local product. In fact, one of the things I like best about walks around Wenatchee is seeing how close to the community the orchards are, right in amongst the residences, filling up the empty spaces, an intimate part of local life.

Two of Wenatchee's famous "sights to see" are not precisely in Wenatchee, but nearby. **Ohme Gardens** is a lush and intricate (and huge: nine acres) garden, even more intense in its use of irrigation than the orchards. It's an alpine garden in a desert setting, and the contrast between the brilliant flowers, verdant growth and quiet pools, and the harsh terrain that surrounds illustrates something of how tenuous and precious water is when it's hard to come by. The view of Wenatchee and the valley from the topmost path alone is worth the trip. Farther north, **Rocky Reach Dam** attracts thousands of visitors to its excellent Gallery of Electricity, art exhibits at the Gallery of the Columbia, and the fifteen acres of garden, park and picnic spots.

PARKS

When I was there in hot weather, the parks of Wenatchee were particularly inviting: places to sit and in most of them a little shade to ease the heat for this native of wet country. **Riverfront Park** especially, because of its proximity to the water, felt cool and peaceful. I kept going back to that place, finding a particular shade tree, panting a bit. **Pioneer Park** and **Triangle Park** are both very near the Apple Bowl Stadium, up the hill west of downtown. Shade trees abound, especially in Pioneer Park, and both are excellent picnic spots, a way of letting the kids out of one's hair, maybe throw the frisbee a little. And I enjoyed the residential walks around these parks. Away from the main thoroughfares it's easier to get a sense of the pace of the town.

For another playground, only without the shade, try **Lincoln Park**, a big grassy playfield with plenty of toys. And for just plain sitting, the square in front of the courthouse has the flower plantings, trees, paths and pigeons that are the attractions of urban parks everywhere.

MUSEUMS & GALLERIES

The **North Central Washington Museum**. recently expanded into the old Post Office building next door. It has expanded its permanent exhibits to include a history of apple growing, as well as an art gallery showing the work of regional artists.

Permanent exhibits in the old wing include the usual scenes from pioneer life, and the not-so-usual working model of the railroad set up to illustrate the rugged route of the Great Northern over Stevens Pass. Some of the other exhibits are equally fascinating: a series of films presents the history of the development of the Columbia River; another film relates the story of the first trans-Pacific flight, which ended right over there in East Wenatchee in 1931.

Work by regional artists is available for purchase at the **Little Gallery** right in the downtown shopping district. A more recent addition to the exhibit space available for artists and printmakers is the **Wenatchee Gallery**. If you happen to be in the area during one of the major regional exhibits at the **Gallery of the Columbia** at Rocky Reach Dam, you are presented with an overview of what's going on in North Central art, and can discover specific artists for further interest.

SHOPPING

Small cities like Wenatchee everywhere are being reborn from the inside. Downtown you can see signs of the new energy emerging in revitalized buildings and the shops that go into them. A good example, and a good place to begin a shopping tour of Wenatchee, is **Mission Square**, a cluster of small buildings restored to the clean lines of their 1930s architecture. The focus is Steven's Restaurant and a couple of shops that seem to fit its stylistic bent. **The Cellar** is a wine shop and delicatessen where you can pick up fine regional wines or the makings for a picnic. The **Green Turtle Boutique** next door displays current fashions, many of which are one-of-a-kind handmade items.

Walk down 2nd Street to Wenatchee Avenue and begin a shopping tour of downtown businesses with **The Final Touch**, where you'll find a selection of handcrafted glass and pottery by Northwest artisans, tucked in amongst more standard gift items. Across the street at the **Country Quilt Shop**, you'll find one of those specialty stores that become more intriguing the more you browse into the intricacy of the form. Next door, the **Homestead Bookstore** maintains a loft in the back with a good representative collection of local and regional history, anthropology, and the like.

Antiques are always a good way to see (and even purchase) a little of the history of a place, and Wenatchee has several antique shops. **Heart's Desire**, with its mishmash of varied collectibles, is one of those places worth a visit on a browse. **Addie's Antiques** has a splendid collection of china and glass, and the **Pretentious Antique Company**, housed in a little Victorian loaded with intricate ornamentation, collects and sells silver, jewelry and antique Americana.

If you're looking for apples and other fruit, you'll find the roadside stands outside of town on the main roads (only in season), but you can be sure of finding apples year round at **Skookum Retail Sales** or at **Wells and Wade Fruit Company**. This report would be unfair to the region if it did not mention a tour of the **Aplet and Cotlet Kitchen** in nearby Cashmere, where you can get a free taste of the candy that's mentioned in the next breath by a lot of folks when they speak of this part of the state.

A NIGHT ON THE TOWN

Travelers and visitors often have a hard time finding things to do at night in an unfamiliar city, especially when the local newspaper and the events calendar and the bulletin boards offer nothing in the way of a performance or a big event. I mentioned the **Liberty Theatre** as part of the historic buildings tour: you might want to take in a movie at this showpiece, and see the ornamental interior in its proper light.

In the performing arts, the city hosts the **Wenatchee Valley Symphony** and the **Wenatchee Civic Ballet**, which play their usual seasons between October and April. They give you an opportunity, since tickets are relatively easy to come by at short notice, of participating in that lively involvement a smaller city sometimes shows toward its cultural resources. In the same vein, look for announcements of performances by the **British Brass Band** and **The Big Band**, swinging those old dance tunes. Call **Allied Arts of Wenatchee** to check on different possible events of particular interest.

Other possibilities include the lounges, usually in the restaurants and motels. One scene that I like is the country and western music at **Murphy's**, where you can really get in and rub elbows with the local folks. Others, with different musical styles presented, include **R.B. MacGregor's** and **Covey's**. With a pal it can be fun to barhop a bit (and on those mellow hot summer nights walk back to the motel). The ski set is said to frequent the **Orondo**, and another kind of crowd, a mix of locals and travelers, might be found hanging out at the **Chieftain's Lounge**, a local favorite.

INDOOR & OUTDOOR SPORTS

One of my first discoveries when I set out to take a closer look at Wenatchee was the **Ice Arena** where you can either go skating yourself (if unlike me you know how to) or watch ice hockey games in season-- the newspaper is full of ice hockey in the winter. As research progressed, of course, I found that many other Eastern Washington cities sport ice arenas, so apparently they are only a rarity on the wet side. There is a roller skating rink (I do know how to do that) as well, the **Wenatchee Roller Skating Center**.

The primary winter recreation around Wenatchee is skiing, and nearby **Mission Ridge**, about 13 miles south past Squilchuck State Park, is popular with both downhill (for the variety of the slopes) and also crosscountry skiers; the season runs from about mid-November to mid-April. Squilchuck Park itself, although it has no ski slopes, is an excellent winter playground, for sledding, snowshoeing and fooling around. A shop that caters to winter sports participants is **Asplund's**, outfitters for crosscountry skiers, mountaineers, hikers and associated outdoorspeople. They also offer instruction in crosscountry skiing.

In the milder seasons white water river rafting is a constant draw, the Wenatchee being considered one of the finest stretches of white water around. Rafting companies in nearby Leavenworth and Cashmere can make arrangements for excursions.

Pioneer Park has lighted tennis courts for evening play, and a couple of blocks away the high school has eight unlit courts. The city of Wenatchee maintains an outdoor swimming pool, and there is a superb (so they tell me) public golf course a few miles out of town, **Three Lakes Golf Course**.

BIG EVENTS

Through the late summer and into the fall the big yearly event is the harvest, when Wenatchee burbles with activity, kind of a festival in itself. In the spring the blossoms take the show, and Wenatchee responds in kind with the **Washington State Apple Blossom Festival**, held for eleven days beginning the last Thursday in April. The huge grand parade, with as many as a hundred floats, bands, horse clubs and precision drill teams, is held the first Saturday in May. Other related events include an arts and crafts and foods fair, the Family Olympics (like a gigantic version of those family reunion games we used to play in Carnation)-- imagine a festival running for eleven days, and think of the variety of interests you might find. It involves everybody. All this *besides* the apple blossoms themselves. If you catch it at just the right time of the year the Wenatchee Valley is almost too beautiful to bear.

And don't overlook another major event that takes place during the festival. The **Ridge to River Relay** draws hundreds of runners and thousands of spectators on the last Sunday of April.

In mid-June, the **Whitewater River Rodeo** attracts sporting crowds for canoe, kayak and raft racing, plus all the other performances and other general fun that go along with a big sporting event. The end of July brings the **Wenatchee Youth Circus** together in the first performance of its summer tour. And come the middle of September Wenatchee hosts the **Apple Valley Arts Festival** along its downtown streets-- it's a big street fair that includes art exhibits, crafts booths featuring some technical demonstrations, and performances by visiting music and drama groups. The **Visitor and Convention Bureau** publishes an events calendar of exact dates.

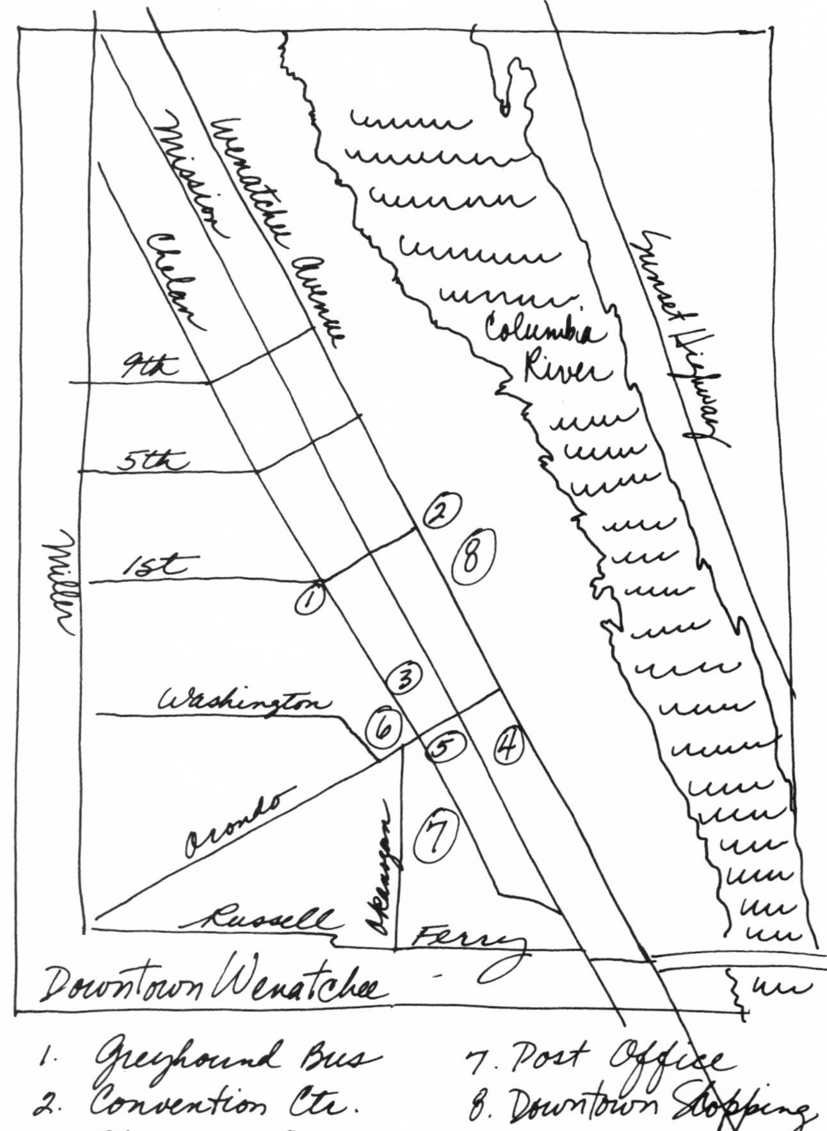

1. Greyhound Bus
2. Convention Ctr.
3. Chamber of Commerce
4. N. Cent. Wa. Museum
5. YMCA
6. Courthouse
7. Post Office
8. Downtown Shopping

Wenatchee Index

FOUR SEASONS INN......134
W. 11 Grant (E. Wenatchee)
884-6611

GINO'S PIZZA......................134
334 N. Wenatchee Ave.
663-0048

GREEN TURTLE
BOUTIQUE............................138
206 N. Mission
663-6335

GREYHOUND BUS
DEPOT.....................................130
301 First
662-2183

HEART'S DESIRE..................139
22 N. Wenatchee Ave.
663-6681

HOMESTEADER
BOOKS...................................139
26 N. Wenatchee Ave.
662-7988

HORAN HOUSE
RESTAURANT......................133
2 Horan Road (Hy. 2)
663-0018

HORIZON AIR.....................130
Pangborn Field
884-0514, (800)547-9308

JET BOAT EXCURSIONS
884-9206

LA COCINA..........................133
1650 Grant Road
E. Wenatchee
884-0514

LIBERTY THEATER.............140
11 S. Mission
662-4567

LINCOLN PARK..................132
Between Crawford, Mission
and Methow Street

LINCOLN ROCK
STATE PARK.......................132
884-3044

LITTLE ART GALLERY.......138
110 N. Wenatchee Ave.
662-2512

MAGNUM'S..........................134
1112 N. Wenatchee Ave.
662-9121

MISSION RIDGE.....134, 141
212 S. Mission
663-6543

MISSION SQUARE............138
202-210 Mission Street

MORRIS HARDWARE
BLDG.......................................133
23 N. Wenatchee Ave.

MUSIC THEATER OF
WENATCHEE
124 Benton
662-7814

MURPHY'S
STEAKHOUSE..........133, 140
123 Easy Street
662-7277

NORTH CENTRAL
WASHINGTON
MUSEUM................................137
127 S. Mission

OHME GARDENS..............136
3327 Ohme Road
662-5785

ORCHARD INN.................132
1401 N. Miller
662-3443

THE ORONDO...................140
111 Orondo
663-1018

PANGBORN FIELD
AIRPORT................................130
Grant Road in E. Wenatchee

PIONEER PARK...................135
(SWIMMING POOL)
663-2521

PRETENTIOUS ANTIQUE
COMPANY............................139
328 N. Chelan
663-8221

QUIET WATER
OUTFITTERS
Cashmere
763-3733

R. B. McGREGOR'S............140
1211 N. Mission
662-9812

RIVERFRONT PARK.........135
Bottom of Fifth St.
663-7181

ROCKY REACH DAM....129
663-8121

SECOND STORY................129
23 S. Wenatchee Ave.
662-1508

SKOOKUM RETAIL
SALES..139
Ninth St. at Railroad
662-5783

SQUILCHUCK STATE
PARK..132
884-3044

STEVEN'S...............................133
Mission Square
218 N. Mission
663-6573

THREE LAKES GOLF
COURSE.................................142
663-5448

THUNDERBIRD
MOTOR
INN...132
1225 N. Wenatchee Ave.
663-0711

TRIANGLE PARK....135, 137
(N. Miller and Orondo)

UPTOWNER..........................131
101 N. Mission
663-5816

WASHINGTON STATE
APPLE BLOSSOM
FESTIVAL..............................142
Info: 662-2116

WELLS & WADE FRUIT
COMPANY............................139
Orondo at Columbia
662-6411

WENATCHEE CIVIC
BALLET..................................140
c/o Allied Arts: 662-1213

WENATCHEE COVENTION
CENTER.................................135
121 N. Wenatchee Avenue
662-4411

WENATCHEE
GALLERY..............................138
630 N. Chelan
663-1887

WENATCHEE ICE
ARENA...................................141
Pioneer Park
662-7731

WENATCHEE PARKS AND
RECREATION
DEPARTMENT
663-2521

WENATCHEE ROLLER
SKATE CENTER...................141
1905 N. Wenatchee Ave.
662-7159

WENATCHEE VALLEY
COLLEGE..............................135
1300 - Fifth
662-1651

WENATCHEE VALLEY
SYMPHONY.........................140
1260 Fifth
663-1457

WENATCHEE YOUTH
CIRCUS..................................142
Info: 662-0722, 662-2849

WENATCHEE
WHITEWATER
Cashmere
782-2254

WESTERBERG
PLAZA....................................131
121 N. Wenatchee Ave.
662-1234

WHITEWATER RIVER
RODEO..................................142
662-2116

WINDMILL............................133
1501 N. Wenatchee Ave.
663-3478

WOODY'S CAB
884-0358

Davidson Bldg. 1889.

Ellensburg

Looking for Dry Weather

Driving through the intense rain and slush whipping around the steep hills and peaks of Snoqualmie Pass, the storm holding strong till Cle Elum, enveloping the whole Cascade Range, almost as far as the vast valley of the Kittitas, where the clouds become lean and the rain thins out to a sprinkle, and finally there is sunshine for awhile in the afternoon, the next day promising to be clear. This is spillover rain from a long early spring storm on the west side of the pass and we are looking for some dry weather.

Ellensburg, for us Puget Sound folks, has always been the landmark indicating arrival in the dry country of Eastern Washington. I've been making that run for years, since high school, when it was an adventure for a 17 year old in his first car to take a real trip across the mountains, into this seemingly foreign land. Often as not the run got only as far as Easton or Cle Elum, where we would cruise the streets eventlessly, and then drive home, pretending the old Chevy had more power, speed and good looks than it really possessed. When we ventured as far as Ellensburg we could, if enough quarters remained after the gas tank's share, cruise to one of the drive-ins around the college, for burgers and a real thrill. Ellensburg is one of the old towns of the state, and the preservation of buildings dating from the rebirth of the town, after a devastating fire in 1889, is truly remarkable. Partly it's a function of the dry weather, but more than that, there is a true civic pride in the structures that exhibit the community's heritage. And the refreshing thing about historic preservation in Ellensburg is that the impulse has extended to period buildings more recent than the wild west days. Mentioned below are a couple of excellent art deco treatments of small buildings from the 1930s. Another treat for the casual visitor are the number of interesting old buildings not yet restored that show some of the possibilities for historic preservation.

The broad valley of the Kittitas, once covered with camas, a staple bulb that brought many tribes of Indians here to gather it in peaceful harmony and socializing, has long been range country for cattle horses and sheep, and the traditions of the cowboys of the old west are preserved in the annual rodeo held at Ellensburg every Labor Day weekend for the past 63 years. The rodeo is probably Ellensburg's main claim to fame, and draws thousands of people, and top-notch cowboys, every year to the three-day event. Other sportsmen, too, find Ellensburg a useful base for hunting and fishing. And of course Central Washington University brings visitors and school-year residents.

ARRIVALS

Ellensburg is a crossroads. To the south, Yakima; to the north, Wenatchee; the quick I-90 from Seattle stretches east toward the Columbia, its vast basin, and Spokane.

As you drop out of the mountains east of Cle Elum you begin to notice the changing terrain, from mountains and their coastal climate, to pine woods and then the broad expanse of the Kittitas Valley, the sense of open space heightened by the beautifully kept large ranches. To the east of Ellensburg the prairie opens up and you see true cattle country--horses, corrals, big spreads-- and you begin to see what the town is the center of. Arriving from the east the view into the Stuart Range and the Cascades is often spectacular, especially as it signals the approaching end of a long, flat drive.

I especially like the trip to Ellensburg from the south, up the Yakima River. The river has cut through mighty ridges of volcanic flow, creating spectacular and complex canyons which, in the manner of this arid country, have the look of an alien landscape. The trip between Ellensburg and Yakima along the old Canyon Road, in either direction, is one of the highlights of a trip to this part of the state.

That's arrival by car. If you are traveling I-90 it's easy to whip right past Ellensburg, completely bypassing the town as most freeways do, or to wind up in a motel at the I-90/ Canyon Road junction and never really see the town itself. Yet Ellensburg is a compact and attractive city that is ideal for walking tours, so it's essential to find the center of town and get out of the car.

There is no commercial airline service in and out of Ellensburg, although there are charter services: **Midstate Aviation** can arrange flights to and from commercial fields. And Amtrak doesn't stop at Ellensburg any more, although you can see the once-handsome old depot now boarded up at the foot of 3rd Avenue. So the only public transportation service to and from Ellensburg these days is **Greyhound**, which stops at the north edge of town, within easy walking distance of the center of things and only a block from the big **Thunderbird Motel**. For west-siders (wet-siders?) the bus is an excellent way to make an excursion to Ellensburg. The trip takes only a couple of hours, so there's really no time to get too cramped and bored; the views are occasionally spectacular and riding rather than driving allows you to enjoy them; and you alter your relationship to a place as a visitor when you experience it without a car. I once rode the bus from Ellensburg to Seattle in the fall when the vine maples were at their most brilliant. There was a very interesting woman in the seat next to me, who shared my fascination with the views, and the trip passed quickly.

PLACES TO STAY

If you arrive from the west and get off the freeway at the first Ellensburg exit, the first major motel you come across is the Thunderbird, mentioned above. While it's no Holiday Inn, the Thunderbird gets my vote as the place to stay in Ellensburg.

Thunderbird gets my vote as the place to stay in Ellensburg. The price is right, the location is close enough to town for walking, and the 1950s kitsch art motif is preserved throughout. Try the coffee shop some early morning and you'll see what I mean.

If you're fussy about motels, you might as well proceed to the east side of town where there's a typical freeway-exit complex that offers you a **Holiday Inn** and all of the services you can expect from an easy return to the highway. Another spiffy new motel there on the east side of town near the freeway is **Nite's Inn**. Both of these motels offer what the older places downtown don't-- a kind of predictable consistency (if you've stayed in one Holiday Inn you've stayed in them all). But what they lack is a close touch with the town. Between these places to stay and the city center lies a long stretch of ex-urbia, the kind of fringe development that grows up on the outskirts of any city, especially in conjunction with freeways. Now I've never been too particular about my abode for the night when traveling, and I prefer to be as close to the living heart of a city as I can, so I can feel the ambience of it as much as possible.

A small group of motels just on the edge of downtown Ellensburg provides ready access to the life of the city, although it is true that they have seen better days.**Harold's Motel** and **Wait's Motel** are older places and show it. But proximity to the town and the university recommends them (and the big tile shower at Harold's wasn't bad, either).

For Bed & Breakfast aficionados Ellensburg offers **Maison McCullough**, probably the nicest overnight experience in the area. Operated by the same folks who run **McCullough's Restaurant** downtown, you can count on being well treated and well fed there.

Campers will find quite a number of campgrounds within a short driving distance of Ellensburg, operated by the **U.S. Forest Service**. Call for availability and reservations. Among several trailer parks in and around the city that welcome overnighters is the **KOA Campground**. where hookups and full facilities are available, and you can pitch your tent.

EATING OUT

A pleasant way to begin a visit to Ellensburg (or a nice way to drop in if you're passing through) is to stop at the **Valley Cafe** for lunch, or for brunch and espresso if you arrive early enough. What a wonderful place! I think every city I've visited has one of those places where you feel comfortable just walking into it. It's partly the way they are laid out, to feel open and airy; it's partly the people working there, the way they interact at first contact; and it's partly the overall style of the place (in this case untampered with for decades), what it tells you about itself. The Valley Cafe is like dropping right into a community, friendly neighbors and all.

So you're in Ellensburg now. Plans for dinner might include making a reservation at **McCullough's**, especially if there's anything festive about the trip. McCullough's is considered the finest of the local restaurants, with an eclectic European cuisine, located in one of the more elegant of the restored downtown buildings, the Davidson Building. In nice weather McCullough's, because it is so centrally located, makes a very sophisticated combination of fine dining and a stroll through Historic

Ellensburg.

One of the very popular places is **Cattin's**, which abounds with attractions for both locals and visitors alike. One is the steaks, notable. Another is its being open all night, and yet another is the lounge with its live entertainment.

Because it's a college town you get plenty of opportunities to sample burgers and pizza: if the kids are unruly you can intimidate 'em with a Big John Burger from **Big John's** right near the campus on the east side. The pizza joint I found most appealing was **Frazzini's**.

Special and ethnic cuisines are a little rare, but for an experience in funky Chinese try the **Pagoda NY Restaurant**, one of those big plain rambling places serving functional Cantonese cooking at the right prices. Mexican cooking is represented by **El Charro**. While this restaurant is a little too anglified to suit me, it's no taco shop, and they serve a Mexican style steak that's quite an experience.

My choice for an early morning breakfast is the **Hiway Grille**, an interesting place to stop any time of day, but especially for breakfast, when you find the locals gathering. I don't know what it is that preserves the atmosphere of some of these places like the Hiway Grille. In many smaller towns time gets stuck. Where there is no need to keep up with fads in decor or cuisine, restaurants like the Hiway Grille become like old Levis that fit the wearer and last forever. To visit one of these truly local cafes is to experience a kind of vicarious community, with badinage flying all around the strangers' table, drawing them into it. Mighty good breakfasts, too, I thought.

A QUICK LOOK

Ellensburg is an attractive town, an excellent place for walking, since there's plenty to see in a relatively small space. The old buildings, many of them lovingly restored or preserved, provide a visual interest that's uncommonly rich. Rebuilt after a disastrous fire in the summer of 1889, the downtown section contains no fewer than a score of buildings of historic interest-- indeed, the whole district is on the national register of historic buildings. And most of these old buildings are in an area small enough to see easily on a walking tour. Pick up a map and printed guide at the Kittitas County Museum or the **Chamber of Commerce** and stroll Main Street and Pearl Street between 3rd and 6th Avenues. For excursions further afield (such as to the old Northern Pacific depot at the foot of 3rd, or to The Castle at 3rd and Chestnut) you might want to take your car. Or you might want to catch a ride on the **Ellensburg Equine Trolley**, a horse-drawn coach that plies the streets of the city and offers a fitting and appropriate way to see the sights. The Equine Trolley Co. also offers charter picnics and covered wagon trips if you want to add some unusual activities to your visit.

Buildings from the historic register are one kind of sight to see. But as you walk (or ride) pay attention to some of the buildings from other eras in Ellensburg's history. One of the things that makes a city interesting is that not every building is an antique; not every building is attractive; and some of the historic restoration of fifty years hence lies hidden under the signage clutter, bad paint and commercial geegaws of today. The Four Winds Book Store on 4th and another small building located mid-block on Ruby are careful restorations of small commercial buildings from the 1930s. Because Ellensburg is small, it's easy to see the overlays of urban styles from successive generations, both the bad and the potentially good. As I walked Ellensburg I continually found unusual visual relationships, and sometimes had to go around the same block two or three times. It's in places like this where you can see how attractive a well-planned city could be.

I would start a walking tour at the **Lynch Block**, at the southwest corner of 5th and Pearl, the one building in town that was standing before the tremendous fire of 1889 wiped out every other major building in town. From there you can walk around and look at a period piece-- period, late summer and fall 1889. The beauty of looking at Ellensburg is that the successive "layers" of buildings are so clear-- later architecture is obvious and distinct. That's not to say that every building in town is noteworthy, but they represent true western Americana and some of the restorations are very well done. At the corner of 4th and Pearl you can glance around and see a half dozen or more of the buildings mentioned in the historical guide, and you can head from there in any direction and within about a nine block radius see the core of the rebuilt town. If you care to venture further afield, you might go east on 3rd as far as Chestnut to see **The Castle**, built as a potential Governor's Mansion out of the hopes this sparkly new city had of becoming the state capital, or west on 3rd to see the **Northern Pacific Depot**, now unfortunately boarded up.

On your introductory ramble around town, try to make a little loop out to the corner of First and

Ruby to see the house and yard there decorated by a most inventive, if quirky, mind. You don't often get to see a well-executed example of primitivistic funk art like this, in any town.

PARKS

For a panoramic view of the town, the surrounding plain of the Kittitas Valley, and the Stuart Range, you may want to drive to **Reed Park**, up behind the rodeo grounds. Other Ellensburg parks offer much in the way of sports, as well as picnic spots and a way of creating a break in family traveling. **Memorial Park** has a covered picnic area, and is the site of the community swimming pool. **Riverfront Park** is my favorite of this city's parks: it's located at Carey Lakes, on the Yakima, and gives the kids a chance for some hiking as well as swimming and picnicking. **Mountain View Park** is the most extensive park in town, with a wide variety of facilities.

HISTORY & ART

One of the first attractive buildings I noticed in Ellensburg was the Cadwell Building of 1889, which houses the **Kittitas County Museum**. The museum is open every afternoon except Sundays, and aside from its collection of memoribilia, it is notable for the Rollinger Gem Collection on display there. A curious geological feature of the area is the unique Ellensburg blue agate, and you'll find references to this gem all around town, as well as examples of it in jewelry stores. At the museum you can learn more about this local rock, and see spectacular examples of it in the Rollinger Collection.

The **Ellensburg Community Art Gallery** is another excellent community resource. Located on the second floor of the restored Davidson Building, the gallery is divided into several small rooms (from its earlier life as an office building) and much of it is lit by skylights. The combination of the intimate rooms and the natural light is ideal for looking at art; when I was last there three modest-size exhibits were running concurrently, a nice broad range of media without crowding.

Probably the most famous art event in these parts is the **Annual National Western Art Show and Auction**, held the third weekend of May. And May is a terrific time to travel to Ellensburg. Sponsored by the Western Art Association, the event draws work from over 200 artists, and thousands of pieces are sold each year. The whole weekend event , including the auctions, is free and open to the public. Part of the proceeds from the show benefit a county training center for handicapped adults.

The location of Central Washington University at Ellensburg gives the town access to a broad range of cultural activities unusual for its relatively small size. Rounding out a sturdy visual arts scene, the **Sarah Spurgeon Gallery**, in the Fine Arts Building on campus, shows both professional and student work in changing exhibits. The gallery is open daytimes during the week. The **anthropology museum**, with its permanent exhibits and a brisk-paced traveling series that arrives every month or so, runs an interesting counterpoint to the historical museum downtown. Some of the architecture on the campus is noteworthy, and Barge Hall, the oldest college building, is on the historic register.

In the performing arts, the **Laughing Horse**

Summer Theatre, a joint effort by the community and the university, draws young professional actors and actresses from throughout the northwest to present four plays in repertory during July and August. And for film buffs, check out the classic film series held periodically in McConnell Auditorium. Find out what's playing by watching the bulletin boards on campus.

In the community, other "cultural" services are provided by the **Public Library**, an unusual and attractive building dating. Among other activities, the Friday Night Movies might be worth knowing about. A good example of the cooperation between the university and the town in providing access to the the arts and humanities is the bulletin board at the library.Community theatre is represented by the **Ellensburg Children's Musical Theatre**, performing in March.

Events around town seem to be pretty well publicized, on bulletin boards and on posters generally well distributed around. The Valley Cafe has a good listing right by the door, and you can see a real cross section of the place on the bulletin board outside **Jerrol's Bookstore**.

Another bookstore, worth its own paragraph, is the **Four Winds Bookstore**. First of all, notice the good job that's been done of restoring the art deco exterior, and how that decoration shows what could be done with the whole block of buildings. Next, notice the **Jabberwock Espresso Bar**, attached: good coffee. Next, if you're curious about the cultural ferment of the place, take a look at the collection of local and regional writing, literary as well as broader subjects, with which the Four Winds stocks its shelves. Few cities sport a traditional bohemian bookstore/coffeehouse like this, and it's a real pleasure to select a book about the area and then sit down and look at it over coffee in a window overlooking an interesting urban view.

SHOPPING

For you inveterate shoppers, one item to seek out that makes Ellensburg unique is, of course, the Ellensburg Blue Agate. I went on a quest for this stone in the shops downtown, and found modestly priced jewelery, as well as highly priced, examples of the gem at several stores. **The Etcetera Shop**, a browser's and olde stuff fan's haven, has blue agate jewelry amongst piles of the right stuff. The **Ellensburg Agate Shop** specializes in the stones, and **The Art of Jewelry** displays the effective combination of attractive stones and settings. Another kind of shopping I discovered with an equestrian daughter, was tack shops. Two that I browsed in are **Mills Saddle & Togs**, notable for the sculptured horse, in western saddle gear, that guards the door, and **Three Creek Ranch and Cattle Co.**, out on the south side of town.

And I'll mention a store that I think you should see, even though the kindly proprietors might not thank me for it. The **Recycle Bicycle Shop** has a gallery of old bicycles and other antique toys suspended and mounted and placed among the bicyles for sale ands repair that otherwise fill the shop-- the marvel of the kid in every one of us. I don't know how you can justify hanging out in a bike shop gawking; maybe just a long peek through the windows.

A NIGHT ON THE TOWN

Outside the big motel lounges at the Holiday Inn and the Thunderbird and the nightly club entertainment at Cattin's, the night life of Ellensburg is to be experienced at a few bars that offer weekend entertainment. One good way to find out what's going on at these places is to check in at **Ace Books and Records**, where posters and handbills adorn the windows with news of upcoming performances. If you want to take pot luck, drop in at **The Buckboard** for a variety of country, western and swing music on weekends. **Third Street Station** offers rock and roll, also usually only on weekends, as does the **Hitching Post Tavern**.

Frequent performances take place at the University, so it's good to keep an eye open for announcements; the **Hal Holmes Center** occasionally is the location for events of public interest; and if all else fails, you can check out the Friday Night Movies at the library.

THE ELLENSBURG RODEO

The split-seconds that define the world of the rodeo cowboy are awesome things, especially when you consider the wild and unpredictable critter that forms the other half of this partnership in precision. With the wins and losses riding on such minute distinctions-- a half second either way between a shot at the purse or a ride on the fence-- rodeo cowboys learn a kind of fatalism and humor that is marked in every event of the rodeo day. For the spectator to watch a tough cowboy ride a tough bucking bronco right over the arena fence and then walk away an instant shy of the leading rider, the excitement can get pretty intense. You're watching steer wrestling, bareback bronc riding, wild horse racing and Brahma bull riding, presented at a rapid clip with clowns and drawling pitterpatter to give you a laugh in the spaces. Learning what's going on only takes a few events; soon you're picking favorites and whooping in the pit of your stomachs when a goodlooking cowboy squeezes out eight plus seconds on a bull.

The **Ellensburg Rodeo** is considered one of the top rodeos in the country and several hundred contestants show up from all over the US and Canada -- including the top professionals. Put together in 1923 the rodeo was then and continues to be a superb cooperative effort by the entire Kittitas Valley community. Even the rodeo site itself is rather remarkable: the arena and track are in their original state and on the adjacent fair grounds stands the restoration of a whole small village of early buildings.

One of the things that makes Labor Day Weekend so exciting at Ellensburg is the terrific number of things to do: not only is the rodeo going on the whole time, but at the **Kittitas County Fair**, also running the whole four days, the exhibit sheds alone can occupy this enthusiastic weekend farmer and his kids for hours. There is a large and intricate carnival, and the food concessions are extensive, with many unusual offerings and lots of bar-b-que. Plus the parade. Held on Saturday of rodeo weekend, the Ellensburg Western Parade is one of the best around. The streets are crowded and the huge parade turns the small downtown sector into one mobile variegated mass, as the floats and teams and marchers move down Pine and back up Ruby, the next street over, so that you see the whole parade twice, in glimpses. Combined with the constant flow of watchers on both sides of the street the throng fills up the town.

INDOOR AND OUTDOOR SPORTS

The art auction and the rodeo are the big events around Ellensburg at the beginning and the end of the season, and midsummer's is the **Whisky Dick Triathlon**, the swimming, bicycling and running event that pits 70 teams of competitors against 30 miles of river, prairie and valley flatland, from the Columbia to Ellensburg. The race is held around the end of July every year.

Quite aside from the big draw sports events like the rodeo and triathlon, the Ellensburg area is rich in opportunities for sportsmen. Summer is the time for floating the Yakima, in rubber rafts, canoes, kayaks or even just inner tubes. To equip yourself for this sport, one of the most pleasant to my mind in the region, stop by **Tent 'n' Tube** where you can rent the gear you need and pick up some basic pointers. Two other outfitters to know about are **Sports Elite II** and **The River Excursion**. The other great sport on the Yakima is fishing. What fishing on the Yakima means is fly fishing, for the wild rainbow trout. If you'd like a hand getting started at this gentlemanly sport, you can hire either **Irish's Guide Service** or the **Yakima River Angler** to lead a guided fishing trip on the river.

The high country around Ellensburg brings the skier in winter. From November through May there is skiing to be found near Ellensburg-- some of the terrain is as high as 6200 feet, and relatively easy access as well as good slopes make the skiing-- both downhill and crosscountry-- some of the best in the state. Probably the best way to check out what's happening on the slopes and in the backcountry is to stop at one of the skiing centers at the summit of Snoqualmie Pass, or check in at Sports Elite II, mentioned above, where you can also rent ski equipment.

Other sports such as hunting, horseback riding, backcountry hiking and the like draw devotees to the Ellensburg area whenever the season or the weather permits. If you care to include horsemanship in your visit, you might want to try the **Indian Creek Corral**, a dude ranch that sets up hunting and packing trips with horses, Memorial Day through November.

For sports indoors, year round, the **Kittitas Valley Memorial Pool** provides public swimming and other pool-oriented facilities such as a sauna and an exercise room. The **Ellensburg Racquet Club** has four indoor racquetball and tennis courts available by reservation.

I still like cruising that trip from, say, Vantage on the Columbia west through the Cascades, with Ellensburg and the Kittitas as the focal point on the eastern side, watching the Stuarts and Mt Rainier looming up, getting a good look at a complex variety of landforms, musing on the long human history of that rich valley, from garden center of the native people to the "Robber's Roost" trading post of the days of early white settlement, the disastrous fire and the phoenix of recovery-- and drop into the center of this little town and see cowboys still on the streets, where outdoor work and play are still the way most folks live here. There's a difference from the towns on the west side, the towns one sees day to day, and a quick trip to Ellensburg is still a pleasant way to see some dry weather when the rain gets old.

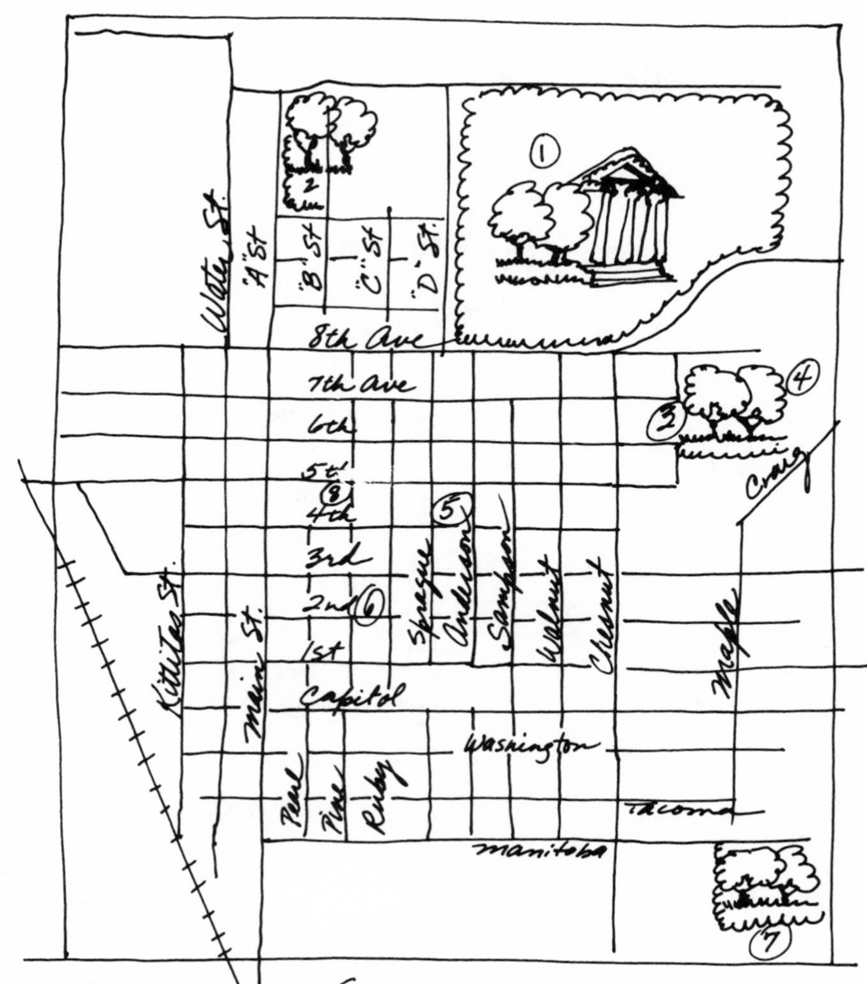

Downtown Ellensburg:

1. Central Wash. Univ.
2. Kiwanis Park
3. Memorial Park
4. Fair/Rodeo Grounds
5. Chamber of Commerce
6. City Library
7. Mount. View Park
8. City Hall

Ellensburg Index

Entrance, Capitol Theater.

Yakima
The Heartland

The Yakima Valley has been under irrigation since the middle of the last century, and the richness of the land, when water is brought to it, is evident not only in the amount produced here, but also in the great variety and sophistication of the growing. The Yakima Indians were among the first farmers, when Catholic missionaries brought techniques of cultivation and irrigation in the early 1850s. Since then a whole mix of cultures has met here, periodically, if only with the harvests and packing.

In the days when commodities were shipped by rail, Yakima was a produce packing and shipping center that drew thousands of workers during certain seasons. With the decline of the railway and changes in the industry, produce shipping dispersed. But even now huge packing houses predominate in a central part of Yakima, and remnants can be seen, as in all the towns discussed, of a greater urban concentration at one time. Agriculture, too, has dispersed over a wider stretch of this country as water management projects, many of them federally sponsored, have opened up new land for cultivation.

But dispersal has meant variation as new crops proved highly successful when attempted. Hops and mint are grown here, as well as most tree fruits, with apples predominating. Most recently the region has been emerging as one of the finest wine countries in America. Driving around is sometimes pleasantly reminiscent of driving the backroads of Sonoma County in California.

The weather is one of the most attractive features of the Yakima Valley, as well as one reason for its phenomenal productivity. With over 300 sunny days a year, so they say, and only about eight inches of rain annually, Yakima offers the visitor about as good a chance for good touring weather as any place in the Northwest.

ARRIVALS

Of the many roads into Yakima, my favorite is down the Yakima River south from Ellensburg. The Yakima is one of the most popular rivers for float trips on the eastern Cascade slope, and during summer months the drive through that strange and mammoth landscape is to the accompaniment of bright rafts and canoes cruising down the river. It's one of those regions where you get a small glimpse into geologic time, for here the lava from countless volcanoes was sedulously cut over and over again by the ultimately more persuasive force of the river. The shapes left by this duel of earth and water are magnificent, and the subtle and intricate play of browns on the dry hills offers a vivid contrast to the green irrigated valley where the river emerges. I always take the canyon road rather than the newer interstate highway. You enter Yakima along the river from the north or south via that interstate system-- Highways 97 and 84 combined-- and if you come from the south you will have seen another spectacular earth/water formation at Union Gap. First Street serves the downtown section, and the main cross street is Yakima Avenue.

From the east down the Naches River you have a chance to see the limits of agriculture as the valley opens out from the foothills and the mountain pines give way to fruit trees.

The **Yakima Municipal Airport** is just at the south edge of town and is served regularly by **Horizon Airlines** and **Cascade Airways**. Car rental is available at the airport, and many of the downtown motels offer courtesy airport service. Actually, it's surprisingly easy to "do" Yakima without a car. For example, you can arrive at the **Greyhound Depot** and find yourself almost across the street from the convention center and a major motel; **Yakima Transit** serves outlying visits such as the museum and west side restaurants, and if it's the wine country you're after, you can arrange a tour from a downtown location.

PLACES TO STAY

Its somewhat central location and the sunny weather here combine to make Yakima a choice for many small regional conventions, and the city solicits that sort of visitors with ample motel and meeting space. The **Yakima Center**, central meeting place for most of these confabs, is flanked by two large motels, **Towne Plaza Motor Inn**, adjacent and, a block away, the **Holiday Inn**, places to know about if you want to find, or avoid, the convention action.

Along N. 1st Street there is a motel strip that is kind of a museum of the form. Try slowly cruising the street a couple of times, and you'll see small, shake-covered motels with round, globe-lit signs from maybe the late 1940s all the way up to ersatz condominiums, with colonial and French Riviera in between. My idea is to stay as close in as possible and find one that matches the car I'm driving. RV campers will find hookups along this strip at **Trailers Inn.** Just outside of town, along the river, **Sportsman State Park** provides camping facilities as well as many recreational opportunities. Aficionados of the bed & breakfast scene may want to check into reservations at **Doniker's**, a place in a residential corner downtown that combines a B & B with a restaurant, more like a European inn, maybe.

PLACES TO EAT

It's a pretty good town for dining, and ready access to the valley's wines makes several of the restaurants worthy of attention. One way to combine several views of Yakima with a lunch or dinner is to visit the small "old town" district of Yakima, along N. Front Street, facing the now abandoned railroad depot. In this row of older buildings you'll find the **Greystone Restaurant** in the recently restored Lund Building, where an acquaintance can be made with the local vintages. Just north along

Front you can see what the right hops can do at the **Brewery Pub**, one of the popular new microbreweries making ales and beers with loving attention to detail. The food is pub style, sandwiches and cheese-- mostly the brew. While you're here, have a look at the vintages offered bottled at **The Wine Cellar**. This is the kind of place that's so useful if you're serious about the valley as wine country. Current expert information, location of wineries, samples and arrangements for touring can all be found here. Along these serious gourmet lines, the fine dinner in a fine old home happens a few miles out of town at **Birchfield Manor**. Serving full-course dinners by reservation only and on weekends only, the Manor has won regional critical acclaim for its classic French cuisine. Similarly, **Gasperetti's** is popular locally with those who pursue formal dining, in this case Italian.

One could do some exploring of cooking styles and national cuisines here. Having lost their fancy digs to a fire a while back, **Santiago's** is not the visual treat it once was, but the eclectic menu still offers up the unexpected. An uptown place downtown is the **Casa de Blanca**, serving nuevo Mexican in a nice-looking upbeat atmosphere. For an interesting mix of Chinese and Japanese, **Haleaina** has its own unusual style, including some Hawaiian dishes and plenty of seafood. There's Irish lamb stew and soda bread at **O'Brien's**. And for some pure Americana, check out **Beth Ann's Ozark's Restaurant and Moonshine Lounge**. The barbeque alone is an experience.

For a lunch right downtown I like **Sammie's Diner** as much for the decor as for anything. I like the views out the round windows of those stable brick ornamented boxes from urban yesteryear. And, yes, you can pick up an espresso on the lower floor of the Yakima Mall at **The Market Place**.

LOOKING AT YAKIMA

As has happened in several other Northwest cities, the business community of Yakima attempted to salvage the urban core by creating a mall, or a mall-like environment. The result is very much like a suburban mall, and it attracts a great number of people to the exact center of town. Whether this method will allow the surrounding city center to preserve its continuity is hard to tell. There are some worthy buildings, and there's a community association actively working on preservation problems. Especially notice the Larson Building on the corner of S. 2nd and Yakima Avenue. It seems like, given the right set of circumstances, something really interesting might happen there. The noble **Capitol Theatre**, with its intricately decorated face, has already been restored by an intense community effort. But separating the restorable district around the railroad depot from the Capitol Theatre is a lot of unregenerated empty space. In the trek between, however, you get a close-up view of the once-mighty produce packing district and in the distance are the surrounding "pretty brown hills". Down the tracks to the south you catch a glimpse of that river-cut notch in the hills called Union Gap. The district of fine older home is to the west, and it's too far to walk; catch a Yakima Transit bus along any of the major east-west streets for loop trips running to different parts of the west side.

To cap off your downtown exploration, in summertime you can hop on the **Interurban Trolley**, restored electric trolley cars from 1906 that zip through the orchard lands and through parts of downtown and the packing district. For getting out into the valley there are several tour services available. Call **Robinson Valley Wine Tours** to find out about tasting trips and other schedules of events in the wine region to the south. **Yakima Valley Bus Tours** also makes arrangements for different trips into the surrounding region. If you just want to be driven around to look at things, try **Classic Limousine Service**.

PARKS

Not long back the city of Yakima developed a big stretch of green land running through the city to provide a great deal of green access for the residents of the place. The 3600-acre **Yakima River Greenway** forms the extensive core of a far-reaching park system that provides extensive outdoor recreation and entertainment. Some should especially be noted because they connect with other destinations in your travels around Yakima. On the west side the well-equiped **Larson Park**, site of many a sandlot baseball competition, lies adjacent to Yakima Valley Community College, where in Kendall Hall many performing arts events are held. Also, the **Planetarium** is located here, something to keep in mind for a special visit. A half-dozen blocks away the Yakima Valley Museum and **Franklin Park**, with its playground, tennis courts and swimming pool are on the same grounds. Farther west **Eisenhower Park** also has a swimming pool. Bus routes Two and Three travel to these west side parks. **Kiwanis Park** and the **Arboretum** are next to one another closer to the river and giving access to the Greenway. And if you're just walking around some of those tree-lined streets you may occasionally come upon a little stretch of one of the many canals that run through Yakima, with an old bridge over it, kind of an unexpected Zen park. To find out where a particular sport or activity is going on in the parks, call the **Parks & Recreation Department**.

HISTORY AND ART

At the **Yakima Valley Museum** you can follow the progress of settlement in the valley through exhibits showing dwellings, household impedimenta and especially transport as the region developed from range country into farmland with the management of water. Another important regional museum is located some distance out of town, but if the history of the place attracts you, it's worth the trip to the **Yakima Indian Nation Cultural Center**. The 20-mile drive brings you to complex of presentations by the Yakima People, including, besides the handsome museum, a gift shop, theatre, restaurant and library. The Yakimas have occupied a central place in the culture of the whole region, with ties reaching clear across the Cascades, for so many centuries long before Europeans came, and they put up such staunch resistance to white settlement when it came, that a long serious look at their culture and history is very rewarding.

Another side of the story can be seen at another museum just a few miles out of town. **Fort Simcoe State Park** has a collection of buildings remaining from the original Army post built here, at the time of the Indian Wars of 1855-57. The cattlemen arrived a year later.

Living history is most vividly seen in the **Interurban Trolley** ride you can take in the summers, and through activities at the **Capitol Theatre**, a community restoration of a fine piece of urban decor.

Art exhibits can be seen at the museums, especially the art of the native culture. Elsewhere, the **Larson Gallery** at Yakima Valley College shows changing exhibits of contemporary artists, both from the area and from the entire Northwest, and the **Yakima Public Library** puts on a variety of exhibits. The **Warehouse Arts Center** houses several arts-related organizations, as well as a couple of galleries, the **Attic Gallery** and the **Warehouse Gallery**, where between the two you can get a look at current regional and local work, as well as traveling shows occasionally on display. Also located here is the **Allied Arts Council** where you can get more specific current information about a wide range of local arts happenings.

SHOPPING

With a shopping mall at the center of the city, most of the stores and shops in that district tend to be focused there, and there's a little less of the sense of strolling street by street looking at things. Businesses are spread pretty widely around the larger city, so browsing those shops is not really convenient for the visitor. The mall tends to have many of the same kinds of department stores and boutiques found in malls in any other place, and the vortex created by shopping mall activity has left quite a number of empty storefronts on the surrounding streets. Still, poking around can be productive. There's a good used bookstore, **Cheshire Book Shop**-- in the mall proper there is a WaldenBooks and a B Dalton's-- and as you explore farther afield you'll run across places such as the **Glass Kaleidoscope** with its collection of stained glass and other tinkly objects, and **Dutchi's Collectibles**, souvenirs and many other trinkets to browse at. The empty spaces and the restorable buildings and the excellent weather keep bringing to mind visions of condominiums and the shops and cultural amenities that could turn the existing mall back into a city again. (But what do you suppose could be done with that parking garage?)

PERFORMING ARTS

The key attraction in the rebirth of downtown Yakima is the stately **Capitol Theatre**. Restored by a major community effort in, the Capitol Theatre is home for the **Yakima Symphony Orchestra and Chorus**, as well as host to a large number of performing events throughout the year. I'd start my visit checking the reader boards at the theatre or the newspaper to see if anything's going on there.

Yakima's drama company has its own boards at the **Warehouse Center**. The **Warehouse Theatre Company** is a long-standing community drama group that performs four or more plays throughout the season. Watch also for summer theatre and performing events sponsored by the Center.

SPORTS

The weather being what it is, outdoor sports here are varied and much pursued, by spectators and participants alike. Among the spectator sports thoroughbred horseracings is one of the favorites, and **Yakima Meadows** is the track where it happens, located near the freeway and next to the **Fairgrounds**, another center for spectator sports and events throughout the year. Horseracing season runs in two parts, weekends between mid-February and May, and again from late August through November. Another kind of racing that's popular here is auto racing at **Yakima Speedway** with a season running between March and the end of September.

Participatory sports available around Yakima include just about any you can think of. Most of the parks are well-equipped for sports, with many tennis courts, swimming pools, horseshoe pits, and some special facilities. There's a city-run nine-hole golf course at **Fisher Park**. One sport that interests many people is river rafting on the Yakima, a pleasant easy-going trip through some spectacular country. For raft and canoe rentals and advice check with **Carrot's Rafting Rentals**, a place to begin getting out on the river. The Yakima is also considered one of the best troutfishing rivers around; if you're heading for the banks you might stop at **Gary's Fly Shoppe** for some of the latest fish stories.

BIG EVENTS

Many of the big annual events around Yakima take place at the **Fairgrounds** and include the major **Central Washington State Fair and Rodeo** held at the end of September. Other annual rodeo competitions include the Washington State High School Rodeo Finals in June and a couple of statewide horse shows during the summer. Also in June the spectacular **Yakima Valley Air Fair** gives you a good look at unusual planes and feats of flying.

The annual arts extravaganza is the **Festival in the Park**, sponsored by Allied Arts and held at the

Warehouse Center and nearby **Gilbert Park**. Also held annually in November is the Larson Gallery's **Invitational Photo Exhibition** on the Yakima Valley College campus. Toward Christmastime comes the Warehouse Center's annual **Arts and Crafts Sale** in late November, followed in mid-December by a Christmas Arts and Crafts show at the Fairgrounds.

The **Visitors and Convention Bureau** issues a good guide to the city as well as an annual calendar of events, so you can check specific current dates.

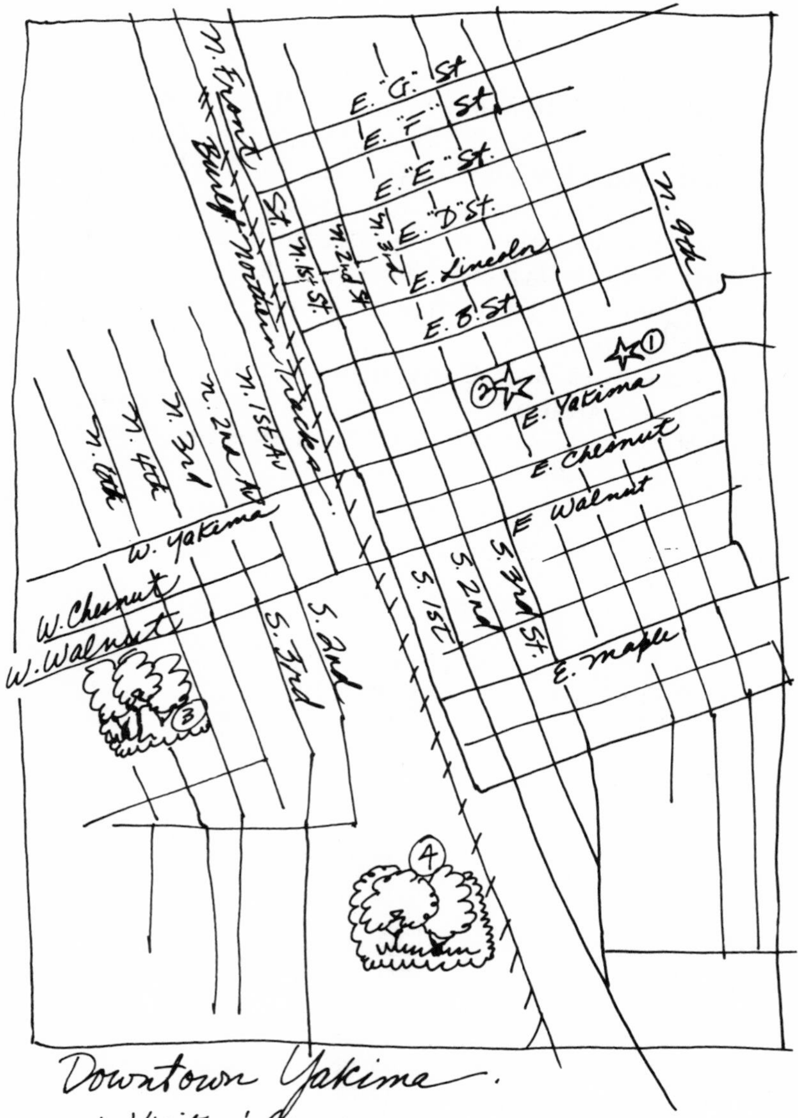

Downtown Yakima.

1. Visitors' Bureau
2. THE MALL
3. Lions Park
4. Raymond Park

Yakima Index

FRANKLIN PARK.................177
S. 21st and Tietan Dr.
575-6035

GARY'S FLY SHOPPE.........181
1505-1/2 Fruitvale Blvd.
457-3474

GASPERETTI'S
GOURMET..............................185
1013 N. First St.
248-0628

GLASS
KALEIDOSCOPE.................179
16 N. Second
248-8507

GREYHOUND.....................169
602 E. Yakima Ave.
457-5131

GREYSTONE
RESTAURANT........................174
5 N. Front St.
248-9801

HALEAINA..............................175
1406 N. 16th Ave.
248-1965

HOLIDAY INN.....................174
9 N. Ninth St.
452-6511

HORIZON AIRLINES........173
Yakima Airport
248-8585

INTERURBAN TROLLEY..176
575-1700

KIWANIS PARK...................177
Fair Ave. at E. Maple
575-6020

LARSON GALLERY.............179
Yakima Valley College
575-2402

LARSON PARK.....................177
S. 16th and Arlington
575-6020

MARKETPLACE....................176
Yakima Mall
457-7170

O'BRIEN'S...............................175
1527 Summitview Ave.
452-7936

PARKS AND RECREATION
DEPARTMENT......................178
575-6020

PLANETARIUM....................177
W. Nob Hill Blvd. and 16th
Ave.
575-2402

RACQUET CLUB
2501 Racquet Lane
453-6521

ROBINSON VALLEY
WINE TOURS......................177
457-7522

Hot Walla Walla Sweets

It was history I was after on my most recent trip to Walla Walla. Looking at the state I wanted to know more about it, and through this lovely valley of many waters passed the earliest incursion of white people into the region. What had stuck from high school was the Whitman Massacre, but it was the Whitman Mission that I wanted to see.

The great fertility of this state is evident driving along the Columbia south of the Tricities then up the rich agricultural land of the Walla Walla River. The great wealth of history, too, pervades the thoughts driving along in the land explored by Lewis and Clark-- and after them the surge of white settlers as before them the steady clop clop of feet and hooves along one of the great native trade routes. On an arrival there at the end of summer a pall hung in the air all across these valleys; hot air turned the irrigation spray to steam; the dust from hundreds of threshers rose along with the smoke from post-harvest burns. The smell of onions and the sense of history. About seven miles west of Walla Walla I stopped at the site of the **Whitman Mission**, now a National Park Service historical monument. The road off Highway 12 passes through fields of asparagus (asparagus!); the site, although no buildings still stand, can easily be reconstructed in the imagination-- it's a small town, really, standing there beside a restored piece of the Oregon Trail. It's a rare piece of archeology to find outside museum walls, and standing on that dusty road in the hot sun I could look east and imagine a white-canvas Conastoga wagon just appearing over the hill; look west, where an abandoned tarmac road once followed the older trail, and imagine pushing on west after the apparent safety of this small familiar place.

You have to imagine the mission compound standing between the road and the river, imagine building houses, school and barns amid the tense excitement of an alien land-- missionaries, yes, but also sign to the native people that great and unwelcome change was coming to their country. What's left now is the historic monument, building foundations marked out with paths amid them and euphoneous talking boxes describing the layout and history of the place. Imagination let loose in a cemetery.

The interpretive center shows what the mute

graves can't, in implements and reconstructions from the site, including the results of the archeology going on there. Books are available giving the visitor a closer look at this land and its role in the western movement.

ARRIVALS

Highway 12 is the primary route into Walla Walla if your coming from the west east or north (off of Highway 125). It runs along the north side of town effectively separating the urban environs from the farmlands other side of the highway. An exit at 2nd Avenue N. puts you right in the heart of town, with motels, restaurants and further forays at your feet. From the south Highway 11 via Highway 25 arrives from Milton Freewater on the Oregon side. Here you are more aware of the sprawl at the edges of the city, but notice that you are in the vicinity of **Fort Walla Walla Park** and the **Fairgrounds** near the point where Highway 25 becomes 9th Avenue S.

Coming into Walla Walla from any directions the traveler is struck by the relation of the fertile valley to the vivid backdrop of the Blue Mountains to the southeast.

Probably only inveterate bus riders (and students) travel to Walla Walla by **Greyhound** and it's rather a grueling trip (several hours from the Tricities, a long hard day from Seattle) but if you take it in little pieces and can stay here and there, it's not so bad. You can connect from regional airports via **Cascade Airways**, and the **Walla Walla City/County Airport** is only a few minutes by cab from the city center. **North American Taxi** serves the airport, along with two other cab companies in town.

If you arrive by public transport you're in luck in that there is an efficient public transit system in Walla Walla,**Valley Transit**, so if you get tired of the close-in walks, you can explore further afield without a car.

PLACES TO STAY

My pick of the motels in Walla Walla is the **Pony Soldier Best Western** primarily because it's close in; I was able to use my room as an effective base camp and move out into the town in easy stages. It's big enough to count on a room except during big events at the college, and the restaurant, recently remodeled, has a nice proprietary feel about it, being off the main path a bit. A similar atmosphere prevails at **The Whitman Motor Inn**, where the adjacent restaurant, **Abraham's**, is both an adjunct to the motel but also a popular place with local dwellers. This place has a touch of history about it as well, being connected to the Whitman Towers, one of the notable downtown structures. On the other hand it is not to my mind as welcoming a place as the Pony Soldier.

On the other side of the college, closer to the highway, there are some other motels you should know about; one, **The Capri**, came to my attention as a place where you could get away from things quietly. Another in this district is the **Colonial Motel**, close to the highway, airport and Eastgate Mall.

Accomodations other than motels are a little on the sparce side; the bed & breakfast fad has not reached the Walla Walla valley the way it has some other parts of the state, and the campgrounds are spread out. However, **Fort Walla Walla Campground** is but a short drive from the heart of town, and is adjacent to some of the most intriguing visitor attractions-- **Fort Walla Walla Park**.

A QUICK LOOK

History pervades a scenic tour of Walla Walla just as it does the nearby memorials. Even the layout of the downtown streets owes its slightly exotic pattern to the vagaries of the ancient Nez Perce Trail, the path of which Main Street was built to follow, it being the major thoroughfare of the time. Standing at the corner of Second and Main you can imagine yourself back in the frontier days and with the dusty trail as the base picture, add successive overlays as the town grew building by building. Nowadays, Main Street curves away from Second Avenue, the apparent downtown center, so you can see some little hint of the way the Trail might have led off toward Spokane. Walking along to the east you find Mill Creek ambling between restored old brick buildings, albeit now constrained in a concrete trench. Here where the trail forded this small river must always have been a gathering place, that grew when white people came into what Walla Walla is as you now see it.

A walking tour of downtown Walla Walla can be accomplished rather quickly, but don't pass up its numerous interesting features just because the urban center seems so compact. To me the most interesting visual quality Walla Walla possesses is that of a frontier community holding out, becoming firmly established against all the odds of the chaos surrounding. Now, of course, both the unruly land and the suspicious natives have been subjugated, but you can still see the remnants of the buttressing and the holding on, in the museums and in the solid brick sturdiness of the modern town.

Mill Creek runs generally east and west, and two of the primary downtown streets, Main and Alder, divide at about the city center and run on either side of the creek, around the grounds of Whitman College. So the town plan is rather confusing, but is also much more intricate and interesting than a city laid out foursquare along a meridian. Saving the Whitman College campus for a later tour, a quick look at the town would involve a walk along Main to the northeast as far as Park Street S., where you turn right (south) and skirt the college campus until you reach Alder Street E. Turn right again and follow Alder to 4th or 5th Avenue S. Turn right again at Main and complete the loop, taking in the **Dacres Hotel**, a national historic landmark. Along this walk you'll see a dozen fine examples of turn-of-the-century urban architecture, including the former **Carnegie Library** (now a center for the fine arts) and the **Liberty Theater**, with its wonderful whimsical facade from the vaudeville days, built on the site of the first structure in Walla Walla (a military fort and barracks), established right where the Nez Perce Trail crossed Mill Creek. Some of these buildings have been in continuous use since the 1880's and 90's, and they provide a visual backdrop for the history of the region. A short walk along Colville Street will take you to the **Kirkman House**, a fine example of period domestic architecture that is also a museum. There is a unity of style that runs through the early architecture of Walla Walla, and as the weather is kind to buildings in Eastern Washington, even unrestored and unpretentious buildings from the early days are well preserved. So attentive touring is well-repaid in the unexpected appearance of handsome brick- and stone-work, decorative cornices and other ornamentation.

To return for a moment to your first walking tour, I think it is worth noticing the way tree-lined streets and sedate older homes, especially around the college campus, give way to long vistas of valley and prairie, especially as you emerge from the town on the south side, with distant views of the Blue Mountains when the weather is right. The contrasts are intriguing, and they give you a sense of how the place is established within a rather vast landscape.

EATING OUT

One of the favorite places I discovered in my explorations of Walla Walla was on that first early morning walk in search of coffee and that silent, just waking intimacy of a place that can only be found before the day begins. Right near the angle of Main Street, where the beginning activity of the town can be seen up close, sits the **Merchants Ltd.**, a sidewalk cafe and delicatessen serving espresso at 6 am and fresh bagels worth waiting around for (and a second cup of coffee). The place is filled with goodies; the bakery is right there visible in the back, the smells almost too tempting for a dedicated bagel eater; the folks are friendly; and it's a great pleasure to sit over espresso outside before the day gets hot, watching the town wake up.

Walla Walla is a college town and many of the eateries are set up to serve college students: lots of burgers, sandwiches, fast food, pizza and beer.

If you're traveling with your kids, they'll love it. The best of the lot, to me, are the pizza parlors. Try **Pepe's**, where the pizza comes in several different styles, and you can build a disc a little out of the ordinary. For burgers, a drive-in right out of the movies, complete with car service, is **Mr. Ed's**, where you can get a breakfast at 5 am; another burger place the college crowd seems to frequent is **The Ice-Burg**.

Speaking of breakfasts, most of the major restaurants open early enough that finding breakfast isn't a problem, and there are a couple of all-nighters for the insomniacs-- most notably **The Red Apple**, a good-old-boy hangout right in the heart of town similar to The Spar in Olympia or The Sportsman in Yakima, where you can buy a cigar or a newspaper or a beer as well as a meal, or sit long over a coffee any time of day or night listening to the locals swapping lies. Finding an *unusual* breakfast can be a problem-- if you want to take a crack at homemade sourdough hotcakes at 6 am, stop at **Sarge's Cafe**, an otherwise unassuming place catering to the college crowd.

Dining in the grand manner is a little restricted in Walla Walla: your choices are limited to a couple of good family restaurants and an excellent Mandarin/Cantonese place, with the plain good cooking of the several Mexican restaurants to see you through. **Heath & Co.** is one of those prime rib houses where the fare centers around big pieces of beef, but it has the added attraction of presenting lots of country and western music as its entertainment offering, so the style fits the locale. Another family restaurant receiving good reports is **The Homestead**, where the menu is fairly predictable, but the folks are friendly and the traveler doesn't feel out of place; it's a place my mom wrote home about. If you're from the coast and are longing for seafood, **The Fishmarket** treats fish and crustacea with great respect, and while the ambience may keep it ignored by the critics, it's a place for good eating.

In its decor, serving style and cuisine, **The Golden Horse** is reminiscent of those traditional Chinese restaurants in San Francisco that manage to accommodate tourists and Chinese and Caucasian natives all in the same garish red and gold spaces. The cooking is colorful and sound, the waitpersons appropriately bland, and the decorative booths are ideal for small parties.

A couple of Mexican restaurants in Walla Wall are worth trying: **La Pinata** and **El Charrito** are both unpretentious and serve straightforward, real food.

Finally, a couple of taverns serving meals should be mentioned: **The Blue Mountain** and the **Dacres Saloon** are listed below in the section on night life.

And to return for a moment to your car full of kids, there's a place here in Walla Walla that's not exactly an eatery, but it doesn't seem to fit in any of the other sections in this chapter, and you might find it handy to know about-- so when the kids are hollering for something to do, drive them out to **The Walla Walla Square Ball Stickyless Popcorn Company** and turn 'em loose.

PARKS

City parks are a blessing to travelers, spaces where the pressures of being on the road and away from can be eased, where unlimited free time can be spent in a public space, and where some image of the place can be seen; parks are a good reflection of a community. Walla Walla has a goodly number of parks, offering a noticeably wide variety of activites and services, from museums to campgrounds to outdoor sports and entertainment. The major attraction is of course **Fort Walla Walla Park** with its campground and especially the frontier village and museum. The grounds are extensive, and the shady picnic areas are welcoming on the hot afternoons of summer. In town, **Pioneer Park** has that lovely formality of an older urban park, with its aviary filled with exotic birds, the duck pond, and the amphitheater where every July three weekends of musical performances are presented. At **Veterans' Memorial Park** there is a stadium with a running track and an outdoor public swimming pool, as well as proximity to the public golf course. Smaller parks are spotted around the edges of the city center, and combined with the college campus and the quiet treelined streets, give the visitor plenty of green space to relax in. And in the very heart of town, at the corner of S. Main and S. Third, you'll find one of those pocket parks so beloved by residents of larger cities, with benches and a fountain, and at times a chance for quiet contemplation of the sunny well-kept buildings.

ART GALLERIES

The arts are kept alive and lively in this corner of Washington by a number of galleries and theatres, including those at the colleges. In the visual arts, the **Mill Creek Art Gallery** is sure to attract your attention, being situated in the heart of town, right on the banks of Mill Creek. The gallery represents and displays the work of local artists in one of the attractive restored brick buildings from the turn of the century. Another handsome building, the old Carnegie Library, now houses the **Carnegie Center**, which along with a sales gallery and gift shop, also offers instruction in the visual arts. At Whitman College the **Sheehan Gallery** brings traveling exhibits to the area on a rotating basis.

SHOPPING

Antiques lead the list of shopping experiences in Walla Walla, with a few unusual clothing and gift stores and some foodstuffs such as wines and delicatessen items added in. The **Kirkman House** has already been mentioned as a museum and example of Victorian architecture; the shop there sells some antiques. Interesting for its exotic flair, **Fiasco** describes itself as "not a normal store" and the description suits-- it's a great place for serendipities, including antique clothing. **Red House Antiques**, while conforming more to the expected run of antique stores, offers a fairly wide selection of articles preserved by the dry climate and the century's accumulation of objects in this corner of the state.

Washington wines are a natural for shoppers in eastern Washington, and while Walla Walla is not right in the heart of the new northwest wineland, it is nearby, so many of the local vintages are available here. There is even one small local winery in town: **Leonetti's Cellar** is one place to try if you're interested in regional vintages. **The Merchant's Ltd** has already been mentioned for its deli and bakery, but you should also keep it in mind as a place for a wide selection of wines, both bottled and by the glass. You can assemble a pretty elegant picnic out of the stuff you find here, and if there's an outdoor concert going on, you can look forward to a promising evening.

A NIGHT ON THE TOWN

Short of a bottle of fine red and a concert in the park, where do you go to find a good time after dark in Walla Walla? If it's autumn and the symphony season, remember that the **Walla Walla Symphony**, founded in 1907, is one of the oldest orchestras in the west, and has a reputation for drawing excellent performances from its 80-plus professional and amateur musicians.

If it's not symphony season, however, you have other choices depending on the time of year. During July a musical is performed by **Walla Walla Community College** for three weekends in the outdoor amphitheatre at Fort Walla Walla Park. Other live music is found year round at **Cordiner Hall** on the Whitman CollegeCampus (check the school newspaper and local bulletin boards for events). In town, the several taverns and lounges offer live music in a variety of styles and levels of quality. Already mentioned is the country & western music at **Heath & Co**. Besides its notable sandwiches, the **Dacres Saloon** is one of those nighspots that is interesting no matter what might be going on, whether its live music or just being part of the general fun. The saloon is located in the old Dacres Hotel, a national historic landmark; in its heyday the hotel was also the stagecoach stop and apparently was at the very center of cultural activity in the old days. On the other side of town, the **Blue Mountain Tavern**, an old-style place complete with card room and good cheap beer, offers another look at the local denizens of the night, and whatever entertainments are on tap for the evening.

Live theater enjoys an encouraging popularity in Walla Walla. The **Little Theater**, a community repertory company established in 1944, presents four plays during its season. On the Whitman College campus the **Harper Joy Theater**, an unusual old wooden structure worth seeing for its own sake, is the site of ten student productions during the academic year.

And if all else fails, you can try taking pot luck at the **Liberty**, that quirky old vaudevillian theater built right at the spot where Walla Walla had its beginnings, where Indians had been fording the creek since time before memory.

INDOOR AND OUTDOOR SPORTS

The recreational possibilities in the Walla Walla area are extremely varied and extensive, whatever the season. In the surrounding region the Blue Mountains offer backpacking, trail riding and camping in the summer, and skiiing and other snowbound sports in the winter. Fishing and other water sports on the Columbia, the Snake and other nearby streams are popular, and hunting is rich in the area. Outfitters and sources of information in Walla Walla include **Pete's Sports Shop** and the **Drumheller Co**. Between the two you can acquire the gear you need and round up gossip and expert advice on just about any sport the region offers. For information about conditions in the nearby national forests, call the **Forest Ranger Station**.

Sports within Walla Walla are just as extensive. At the **Veterans Memorial Sports Complex** the sports and exercise facilities abound, and include a jogging track and an outdoor swimming pool. The complex adjoins the public, eighteen-hole **Veterans Memorial Golf Course**. There is another outdoor pool at **Pioneer Park**, and you'll find indoor pools at Whitman College and at the **YMCA**. The Y is used a great deal by the folks who live here, and it is remarkably well equipped; there are courts for a wide range of sports and games, including basketball, racquet and hand ball, as well as a weight room. The **YWCA** has an ice-skating rink, the Ice Chalet, a very popular spot among local residents.

Outdoor tennis courts abound, at the Veterans Memorial and Pioneer parks, as well as Jefferson Park, Menlo Park and a couple of the schools. You can rent bicycles at **Sun Sports**, and have a ride on the bike path along Mill Creek (or on out to the Whitman Mission, for that matter, an easy seven miles west). Ask at Sun Sports for the routes of other bike paths in the immediate vicinity.

At the **Ace of Clubs**, a commercial health club, you can, for a fee, use the indoor jogging track, racquetball and handball courts, exercise machines and other facilities.

BIG EVENTS

Any time you are traveling to Walla Walla, you have a chance of catching one of the many annual events that dot the calendar year round. My favorite is the **Hot Air Balloon Stampede**, held in May, when you can see those silent colorful globes rising majestically over the green valley--it's somehow medieval in its silent anachronistic grace. Moving through the year, summer brings the **Sweet Onion Festival** held in July, as well as the 4th of July in the Park celebration. During Labor Day Weekend you can experience the thrills and spills of the **Southeastern Washington Fair and Rodeo**. Spring brings the **Northwest Regional College Rodeo**, training arena for the professionals that come later on to the big meets throughout the west, in March. April finds the streets of downtown Walla Walla filled with artists and artisans, at the annual **Rennaissance Faire**, drawing thousands of visitors to the display booths and cultural events.

Other events throughout the year include dog, horse and gem shows; swimming, golf and softball tournaments; and marathon racing. For each year's specific schedule, or for more information about the event that interests you, call or write the **Chamber of Commerce**.

If you're just passing through, or are under the stress of visiting a loved one in the penitentiary, Walla Walla may seem a sleepy little farm town. But if you get there at the right time, or if you are willing to dig a little, you find a Walla Walla that has fun in its quiet way, and you begin to see why folks who live here love to be here.

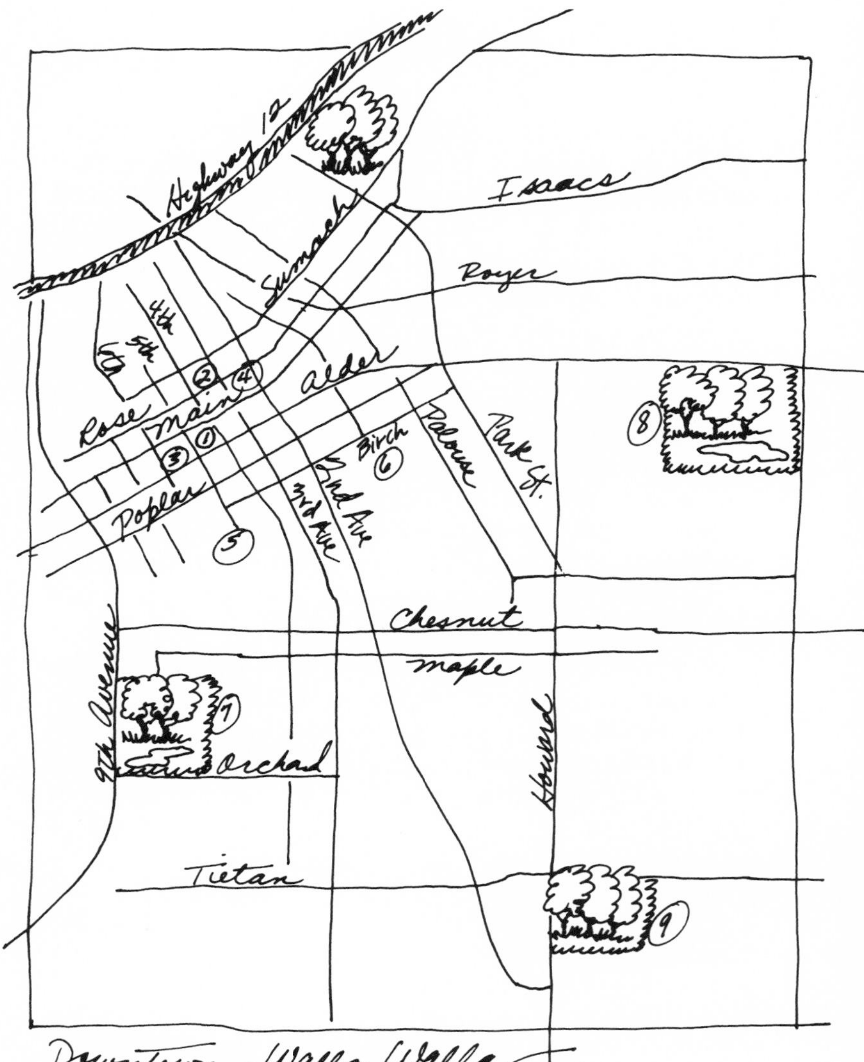

Downtown Walla Walla

1. Dacres Hotel
2. City Hall
3. Court House
4. Greyhound Bus
5. St. Mary's Hospital
6. YMCA
7. Jefferson Park
8. Pioneer Park
9. Tietan Park

Walla Walla Index

PONY SOLDIER BEST WESTERN....................198, 202
325 E. Main
529-4360

RED APPLE............................196
57 E. Main
525-5113

RED HOUSE ANTIQUES............................199
214 E. Main
522-2185

RENAISSANCE FAIRE...203
c/o Chamber of Commerce
525-0850

RODEO EVENTS
Fairgrounds
529-1246

SARGE' S CAFE.....................196
Ninth and Alder
522-1693

SHEEHAN GALLERY........199
Whitman College
527-5249

SOUTHEASTERN WASHINGTON STATE FAIR...........................203
Fairgrounds
529-4170

SUN SPORTS.......................202
527 E. Main
529-9550

VALLEY TRANSIT...............192
8 West Poplar
525-9140

VETERAN'S MEMORIAL PARK...201
505 E. Rees
527-4344

VETERAN'S MEMORIAL GOLF COURSE..................202
201 E. Rees
527-4507

VETERAN'S MEMORIAL POOL.......................................198
505 E. Rees
527-4344

WALLA WALLA CITY / COUNTY AIRPORT.........191
Highway 12

WALLA WALLA COMMUNITY COLLEGE...............................200
500 Tausick Way
522-2500

WALLA WALLA SQUARE BALL AND STICKYLESS POPCOR N COMPANY............................197
630 S. Ninth
525-5333

WALLA WALLA SYMPHONY.........................200
3 W. Alder
529-8020

Pullman and the Palouse

I don't remember where it was that I realized I had entered the Palouse Country, on that trip north of Clarkston somewhere along Highway 195 toward Pullman. I wasn't ready for it that first trip, and didn't notice until I was maybe back in Washington. But I know the Palouse stretches into Idaho, creating a region that in numerous ways transcends the rather arbitrary state line.

The Palouse is a land of undulating waves of top-soil-- a giant puddle of drying mud left by a great flood slopping against the Rocky Mountain foot-hills. Hundreds of feet deep in places, the soil of the Palouse is friable and shifty, the richness of dry land grain farming challenged by the soil's subjectivity to water and air erosion. To the traveler, who sees only the image this fragile balance presents, the land is a constantly and subtly changing work of art in nature; at every turn of the highway the eye re-encapsulates the basic structures of form and color in a view essentially simple, but so variable that the eye is awakened to what a painter often sees. The flat blue sky (but an intense flat blue), the massed shades of brown (but composed of minute changes in tint and hue), are seen in large swathes. Light changes perpetually, and can be seen changing. When a focus for the eye appears-- a cluster of farm buildings, a flatbed and combine moving together along a slope-- the mind frames and composes it as a picture: instant, fugitive art.

In Washington, Pullman is the largest of a number of towns and small cities in the Palouse. In a land that is mostly wheat farms, the population is small and spread out; many of these towns, including Moscow, the major urban center, are on the Idaho side; most of the towns are clusters around grain elevators along a rail line. Pullman, because it is home for Washington State University, is a small city that takes on very specific roles besides shipping grain and serving the farming industry. Because of the University it is a busy place, and, though small as cities go, is graced with historical associations and blessed with contemporary amenities enough to attract the visitor on a short stay.

Located along the south fork of the Palouse River, the town grew up at the confluence of the river with two other streams: Three Forks Ranch, the place was called originally. And you can see how the river dictated the shape and growth of the place as you notice its journey through town and the canyons the town sits in carved from the surrounding hills. Originally used for cattle grazing, the land was turned very quickly into dry land wheat country; the University, dedicated to agricultural learning and experimentation, has been an integral part of the great productivity of the Palouse since its founding in 1892.

Truly a crossroads-- on the map the main arterials look like a four-legged pinwheel-- Pullman acts as much like a vortex as it does a crossing, and the calm community atmosphere of the center off town is constantly being revved up by the four busy streets whizzing around the edges. It's a city that's easy to miss. Even the college students, for the most part, have gone to Moscow, eight miles east across the state line, partly because the legal drinking age was lower. But at the same time a college community is truly a community, a crossroads actually does function as a meeting place, a "bumping into" place, and Pullman shows an easy acceptance of punked-out college students and sedate ranchers sharing the same coffeeshop and icecream stores.

ARRIVALS

If you arrive at Pullman via the roads from Moscow (Highway 270) or Palouse (Highway 27), notice as you approach town the turns onto Stadium Way. These are the main entrances to the University, so you will be returning to them later. If you arrive via Highway 195 from the north or south, there's a tendency when you hit town to get stuck in the vortex of streets and find yourself headed back out of town again in another direction. When I was last there I was aiming for a specific motel and missed it twice before I had the sense to stop the car and get my bearings. But it's not so big that you can get lost.

Two regional airlines, **Horizon Air** and **Cascade Airways** fly regular schedules to the **Pullman-Moscow Airport**. Several of the motels have courtesy service to the airport. You can get a ride into town, and a quick tour of the place if you want it, by calling **City Taxi**. The **Greyhound Bus** stops at one of the most pleasant restaurants in town, the Couger Cafe. Pullman has a small but useful bus system, **Pullman Transit**, especially for rides to the campus.

PLACES TO STAY

Sharing easy access to the center of town along with a view overlooking Pullman and WSU, the **Hilltop Motor Inn** is an obvious choice to settle into for your stay. The excellent dining room adds to the pleasure of living here for a few days. If you want to get even closer in, the family-operated **Cougar Land Motel** is alittle homier than a chain place, and comes closest to that sense of a hostelry in the heart of town. The closest to a hotel experience-- complete with lobbies and elevators-- is the **Compton Union Hotel** right on the campus, used extensively by academic and business visitors to the University. For ready access to the university, the straightahead **Thunderbird Lodge** has some rooms with views, with the Hong Kong Restaurant appended, and is situated right across the street.

RVists will find the **Pullman RV Park** handy to the town and even handier to all the resources of the adjacent City Playfield. Campers will find good facilities and plenty to see and do at nearby **Kami-**

ak Butte County Park.

PLACES TO EAT

Because it's a college town, Pullman has a lot of college food-- different, certainly, in style from the parade of fastfoods in some big suburb-- here the fare runs to tavern burgers and pizza, and fastfood on the exotic side.

For making an evening of it, dining possibilities include **The Seasons**, where you can dine in a fine old home, select from a good collection of Washington wines and take a walk among the old brick buildings & downtown streets. The Seasons offers musical events on a regular basis, too. For Mexican cuisine presented in a pretty grand manner, **Alex's Restaurante** makes a great gathering place for a group, with a lounge attached and good beer. **The Hilltop Restaurant** has a reputation for its steaks and the view, well-deserved for both. And I'll throw caution to the winds and recommend one of the several Chinese restaurants in town, **The Mandarin Wok**, for its good-looking decor and sound menu.

If you're looking for lunch there is a range of possibilities. For something out of the ordinary the **Quick Food House International** will sell you a walking Philippine teryaki and you can continue on your way. A more substantial approach might be **Sam's Old Southern Bar B Que**, where you can also pick up something to take along.

I always like to get an idea about the next day's breakfast, and if you want to get out and get moving you can start at 5 am during the summer at the **Cougar Cafe**, a cheerful place that appreciates breakfast. Another spot I've enjoyed is **The Small Place**, where I spent one early morning overhearing two working WSU graduates in a discussion of wheat combines that changed my whole perspective on farming. And for all kinds of action from breakfast at 5 until cards in the wee hours, the **Station Restaurant** might be your place.

If treats are your line, you won't make any more jokes about the cow college after you've tasted the ice cream or cheese at **Ferdinand's**. The limited hours (10 - 4 weekdays) might be a problem if you're just passing through, but a visit is worth the effort. Find an espresso place and you're set: **The Combine** has coffees and pastries for a continental breakfast or tea.

LOOKING AROUND

Get up on the hills around Pullman and you are in wheat country, and there are various promontories where you can look at the bowl of the river and town, the commanding place of the university, and all around you those undulating hills. The walks seem long, but it's great bicycle country, if you can handle the hills, and cruising in the old Chevy is of course heaven.

The town itself is small enough that the car's a nuisance, and a walking tour can be both pleasant and fairly comprehensive. Once you've isolated some landmarks and major streets, you can become deliberately lost among the jumble of residential streets. When a street (usually a main one) looks too long or dusty, turn onto a side street and let it lead you on a circumambulation of the town. Turn-of-the-century brick buildings downtown interest me most, and the occasional fine old home seen in residential wanderings. The river and the several parks appear if your walk goes on long enough, as do hills you may want to skirt or climb for the chance at a view.

Built in 1890-92, the WSU campus provides a walk among historic buildings, showing the growth of the university, one that you can adjust to your energy or interest. A good central place to begin is the Compton Union Building, where but a short walk brings you to Bryan Tower with its clocks, the central focus of visual interest on the campus. Try to make your walk extend to the Physical Science Building, where its thirteen floors are the most spectacular viewpoints in the vicinity.

PARKS

For size, river access and number of activities, the **City Playfield** is probably the primary park in town, especially if you've landed in the RV Park. Two others to keep in mind are **Reaney Park**, where the swimming pools are; and **McGee Park** (*), off Stadium Way on its sweeping drive past the campus, for the play areas, the views and other features. With its proximity to the river, **Neill Public Library** has something of a park-like setting, and an unusual view of the town. The new **River Park** gives even more access to the Palouse along with its other amenities.

And, in your walking visit, don't ignore the little urban pocket park at the foot of High Street--well restored buildings and shaded benches blocked off somewhat from the busy streets, therefore quiet and a rootbeer float or a beer not far away.

MUSEUMS & GALLERIES

Pullman doesn't host the kind of city museum,

run by voluble volunteers, that is the mainstay of dedicated tourists. Given a little nudging the whole place could become a kind of open-air museum, with implements and displays added to refurbished old buildings. The weather's right for it. An example of what's possible is the series of colorful murals on the street-level boarded-up windows of the **Moose Lodge**. The place to see museum collections of several different kinds is the university. The anthropology department at WSU is notable for its work in the prehistory of the Northwest, and the **Museum of Anthropology** reflects the level of that dedication. The **James Entomological Collection** is the largest collection of insects in the Northwest. And the **Museum of Art** contains the Drucker Collection of Oriental art as well as rotating exhibit space, where the bring in some important shows.

Downtown art galleries include **A Fine Line** and the auxiliary **Watercolor Workshop** operated by the local artists guild. Nearby, **Nica Gallery** exhibits local and regional artists' works.

SHOPPING

A stroll north along Grand Avenue from its intersection with Main will give you a brief shopping tour, taking in the art galleries mentioned above. Across from A Fine Line Gallery, **Brused Books** sells both new and used books, and has a respectable selection of regional material. Across the street again and further along, **The Old Mole** sells handmade objects and artifacts. Next to The Couger Cafe, **Blue Moon Antiques** has enough mysterious objects out of the region's past to intrigue any explorer in curiosities.

NIGHTLIFE

Well, you know college towns: loud taverns with big sports screens and beer, shuffleboard and pool. A couple of them, **Cougar Cottage** and **Rusty's**, have been operating here since the 1930s, so are institutions worth checking out if only for the tradition (as long as you're not a UW fan). A little more grownup version is **The Station**, with a restaurant and cocktails as well as the big screen, and gambling to put a little kick into the evening. You might also check out the supper theatre offered by the **Hong Kong Restaurant**.

Many of the theatrical and musical performances that go one here happen at the **Beasley Performing Arts Coliseum**, where the huge hall holds thousands for sports events and the theatre is used for concerts and drama. Watch for performances of the **Washington Idaho Symphony Orchestra**, as well as traveling groups and performers.

The campus is a good source of entertainment any time during the school year. One of the places theatrical performances are often held is the **Daggy Theatre**. In the summer the WSU **Summer Palace** is a popular series at Daggy Hall. Other, smaller halls are used for a variety of films, readings and lectures. Check bulletin boards at the Compton Union or the campus daily newspaper for immediate announcements. Another bulletin board to have a look at is outside **Rico's Smokehouse** near the corner of Grand and Main. One organization you might watch for is the **Pullman Community Theatre**, a mainstay of theatricals for the past 35 years.

SPORTS

Most of the usual sports activities are available to the Pullman visitor with, again, the WSU campus providing many of the facilities, especially in spectator sports. The Coliseum hosts sports events throughout the year: check schedules. The **WSU Golf Course** is a nine-hole layout with driving range, open to the public. Call the **WSU Recreation Department** to find out what facilities may be open to visitors.

In town, the swimming pools are at **Reaney Park**; other sports faciltities are spread out in parks around town, many of them in the **City Playfield**. Call the **Parks & Recreation Department** for locations and use arrangements for your favorite sport.

If you're looking for gossip and advice about sports further afield in the Palouse country, **Blue Mountain Recreation & Cyclery** is Pullman's primary outfitter for skiing equipment, whitewater rafting, camping and the like, and you can rent bikes here. You can get a lead from these knowledgeable folks before you head out into wilder country. For conditions and reservations at regional parks, call the **Whitman County Parks Department**.

BIG EVENTS

'Tis spring in Pullman and the mud is wonderful. That's what they call the annual April celebration of the end of winter and the coming of the spring mud: **Mudwonderful**. In a less whacky tradition, Pullman's **Fourth of July in the Park**, an old fashioned, all-day community picnic in Sunnyside Park, has a good old pyrotechnic display as the finale. Later in July the whackiness crops up again at Pullman's **Crazy Days**, a midsummer romp celebrating the town's birthday. In the fall, **Harvest Fest**, held every September, draws crowds to the downtown streets. For specific dates of annual events call the Pullman **Chamber of Commerce**. The school year brings its annual round of activities to WSU; to find out about sports and other activities call the information number at the university.

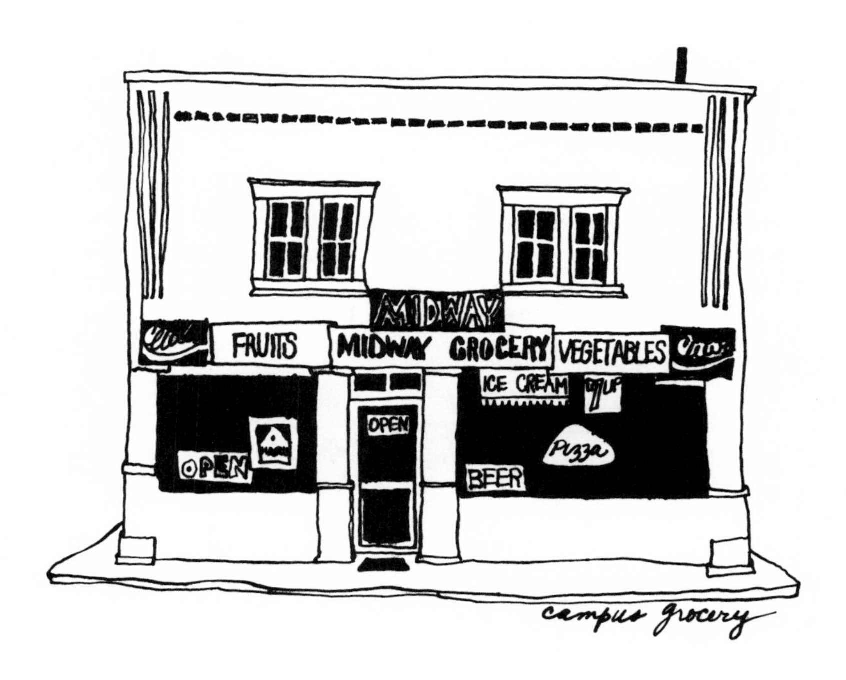

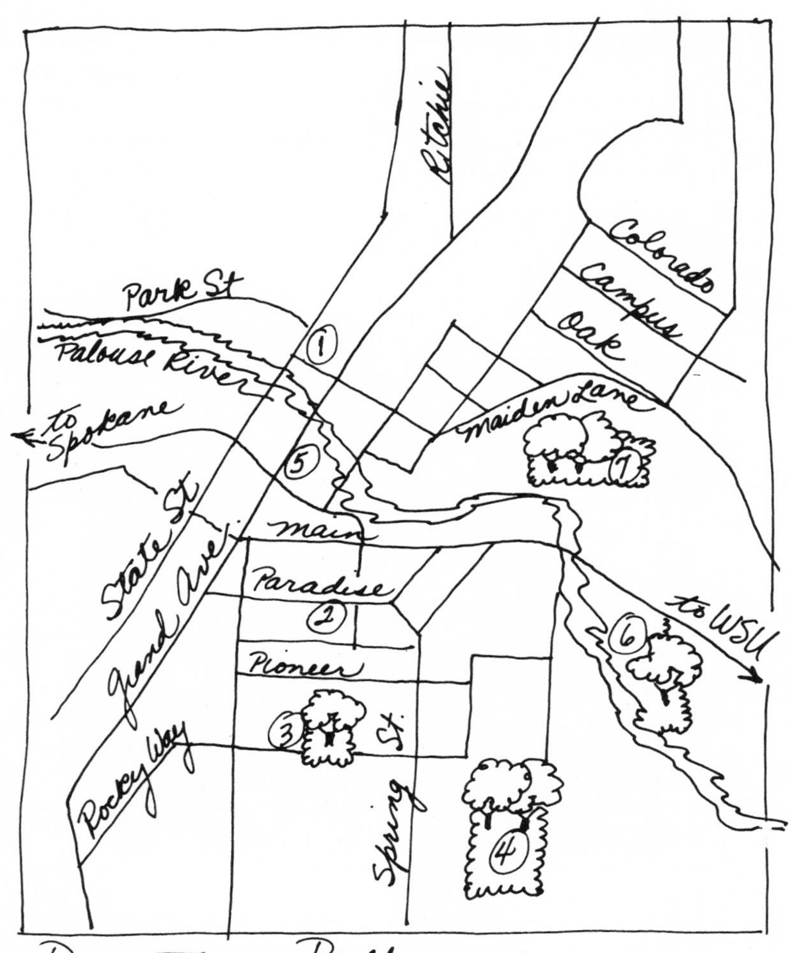

Downtown Pullman

1. Chamber of Commerce
2. City Hall
Woodcraft Park
4. Kruegel Park
5. Library
6. Playfield
7. Reaney Park

Pullman Index

HONG KONG
RESTAURANT......................217
S.E. 915 Main
334-5550

HORIZON AIRLINES......212
Pullman-Moscow Airport
334-1877

KAMIAK BUTTE
COUNTY PARK..................212
Rt. 27
878-1869

MANDARIN WOK............213
N. 115 Grand
332-5863

MAURICE T. JAMES...........216
Entomological Collection
Johnson Hall
WSU Campus

McGEE PARK.......................215
Lybecker Rd. at Upper Dr.
334-4555

MOOSE LODGE.................216
S.E. 150 Kamiaken
334-3000

MUSEUM OF
ANTHROPOLOGY...........216
College Hall
WSU Campus
335-3441

MUSEUM OF ART.............216
Fine Arts Building
WSU Campus
335-1910

NEILL PUBLIC
LIBRARY.................................215
N. 210 Grand Ave.
334-4555

NICA GALLERY 216
N.E. 125 Olson
334-1213

OLD MOLE...........................216
N.119 Grand Ave.
334-2401

PULLMAN COMMUNITY
THEATRE................................217
332-6538

PULLMAN MOSCOW
AIRPORT..............................212
Airport Road via Main

PULLMAN PARKS AND
RECREATION 218
S.E. 325 Paradise
334-4555

PULLMAN RV PARK........212
S. Riverview at City Playfield
334-4555

PULLMAN TRANSIT........212
332-6535

Spokane
le boulevardier

Traveling north from the Palouse country the terrain turns more rugged; the cultivated rolling hills give way to a rocky, ravine-marked, sparsely tree covered land. You're on the craggy edges of the giant puddle, marked by the ravages of that ancient flood that shaped much of the interior of Washington at the end of the last glaciation. That's geology. Historically, Spokane was a place central to the Indian trides of the region. Started as a fur-trading post, it grew because of several mining discoveries and booms, stabilized with the arrival of the railroad and settled in. These days, arriving from the west on I-90 you crest the hill above town and are presented with the panorama of Spokane spread out before you, a sprawling city of over 170, 000 people, the major metropolis of what is known as the Inland Empire, which stretches from the Cascades to the Rockies.

As you travel around the Spokane area, evidence of the (comparatively) long history of the place is all around you-- from the nearby ancient pictographs on the Little Spokane River and the interpretive center at the site of Spokane House, the lively focus of early trading activity between whites and Indians, to remnants of the great Mullan Road seen from the Inland Empire Highway. Governor Stevens is thought by many to have signed an important treaty with the Upper Spokans under a particular tree a few miles east on the Bigelow Gulch Road. Our history in this part of the world is relatively recent, and the remnants of it are still pretty clear. But the history of the people we found here goes back to time of the great flood and the retreat of the last glacier. And the important thing is, you can find evidence of that history, too. Sparcer, certainly, but in travels around Spokane you can get a sense of the movement of white culture into the culture that went before-- all the way from the most obscure writing of prehistory to the whizbang facade of a multistory downtown parking lot.

In downtown Spokane most of the visible history dates from the disastrous fire of 1889, the year so many Northwest towns burned. But the buildings you see dating from the 90s and thereafter illustrate a kind of exuberance that has been nicely preserved here, making the city architecturally one of the most interesting in the state. Spokane, to me, illustrates very well the potential rebirth of cities. For in 1974, when Spokane held its world exposition, a huge area of railroad yards along the river was cleared away to make room for the fair, and the resulting facelift seemed to boost the town's spirits as well as its appearance. Now, a walk around Spokane shows a nice blend of that peculiar out west version of Victorian building, sturdy commercial edifices from every succeeding generation, and futuristic glimpses of what the urban environment might look like as cities begin to live again.

I like Spokane. It's almost the ideal place for folks like myself who like walking the streets of a city. There's enough excitement on the streets and just enough hint of roughness to keep you from letting yourself get bored-- yet people are so friendly here that it's hard not to jump right in and get involved. A quick walk around will show you, as if in a display, the panorama of an American city just going into its second century-- the gutterish side as well as the glamorous. The Skid Road elements are necessary, or inevitable, to a city, if only for visual relief from the relentless middle class. On the other side, it is the only city I know in the state that has as its downtown center a park, and some of the ritziest social scenes around go on right here. Spokane is a microcosm of the urban scene and shows to us in a way that larger cities can't, what a city really is and what, in our best hopes, it could become.

ARRIVALS

For most Washingtonians the arrival into Spokane is along Interstate 90, the other major highway in Washington besides I-5, which hooks Spokane by a long concrete ribbon to Seattle. I've already mentioned the view you have on a good day of Spokane as you drop down into the valley of the

Spokane River along the I-90 approach to the city. You can look right out into the mountains of Idaho, where much of the city's wealth came from. You can see the city contained by its suburbs, the core of it clustered by the river. It's a wonderful view if you catch it right, and worth finding a secluded overpass for a liesurely look.

If you drive into town from the north (Highways 2 and 395) or the east (I-90), you cross the broad valley that Spokane grew out into. The suburbs spread out to the northeast from the bowl formed by a curve of the river. Until you arrive at the river's edge along these routes, you could be on the edge of any large town or city anywhere in the country. As in all these situations, my suggestion is to get off the main route or freeway, get as close to the center of town as you can, and park the car. Wherever you go from there, to hotel room or out for a walk, will be a better experience of the town than arrival by freeway.

The **Greyhound Bus Depot** is located a short walk from the very heart downtown Spokane, so if you're arriving by bus, you can stash your stuff, walk north and east and find yourself on a made-to-order walking tour filled with history, architecture and street life. While the Davenport Hotel was in flower, the bus traveler was plunked down almost next door to that elegant hostelry; still, you can haul your stuff to the Ridpath.

Amtrak, too, serves the old Burlington Northern Depot on another edge of the urban core. You can see how transportation and commerce and "street awareness" have changed and where they've gone. When we get around to recreating the cities, we'll start at the train and bus depots. Arrival from the west by rail on the daily *Empire*

Builder is reminiscent of the great continental flyers of yesteryear, and the high rail bridge sweeping into town gives a certain grandeur to the view of the city lights you see laid out before you as you come into town.

Arrival by air is via a number of major airlines, as well as several regional ones. **Spokane International Airport** is a few miles to the west, near the junction of Highways 2 and 90. Taxis normally charge $12 for a trip to or from the airport to the downtown hotels. Call **Lilac City Cab** for pickup or information.

GETTING AROUND

Spokane is a city of busy one-way streets and major multi-lane suburban boulevards. If the traffic seems a little racy, remember that this is a racing town: auto and drag racing and before that the horses; horses still, and before white settlers, Indians raced around here, too. Anybody with big urban car savvy soon fits right in, but it's all too easy to slip into the auto mode of tourism, and Spokane, while it can be seen best in a short time by car, offers rewards for the walker that shouldn't be missed.

Streets are numbered in the four directions from a central point at Sprague and Division. One peculiarity is that the directional indicator always precedes the street number in addresses (i.e., W. 111 Sprague); and if you ignore those directional indicators, you are lost. The river and the freeway chop up the north/south streets , but if you remember that the river cuts the streets north generally between 700 and 1000, and the freeway cuts the streets south at about 400, you'll soon stop crossing the river or going up the hill inadvertently. Sprague and some of the other streets east go on forever.

The city bus system, **Spokane Transit**, operates an efficient series of routes like spokes from a kind of central hub at the corner of Howard Street and Riverside Avenue. Between the Skywalk and frequent bus schedules right downtown you should be able to get around comfortably in inclement weather. You will want to organize your forays afield starting and returning at that central transfer point.

PLACES TO STAY

How you orient your visit to Spokane will depend a lot on where you decide to stay. (That's not so true of other cities.) If you decide on a fancy hotel near the performing arts center you will experience Spokane differently than if you stay at a motel near the freeway into town. Accommodations range from the Sheraton to the shabby, priced accordingly, with excellent hotels and motels at appropriate rates in between. The Bed & Breakfast trade is brisk. RV and camping facilities, including resorts, dude ranches, radiate out from the edges of the city in all directions: the wilderness starts right nearby. So your choices are plentiful, but you might want to pause and think about the first night's lodging before you get caught racing around Spokane's freeways and big one-way streets.

I should mention first off that the Davenport, as of this writing, is closed. When I first started going to cities deliberately, one of my plans was to stay at the elegant old **Davenport Hotel** in Spokane, which I had heard about from friends and read about in guides and histories. Alas, not long before I had my chance (spring of 1984) the Davenport's doors were closed, so a connection that visitors could have had with the splendid days of gold rush and big money around Spokane is not, at the moment, available. A group called **Friends of the Davenport** is working valiantly to let Spokane see the Davenport come alive again; perhaps you can support them in some way.

I wanted to get that sense of excitement one gets staying in a big downtown hotel-- they're hard to find in most smaller towns, changed into apartment buildings mostly. And of course urban centers have changed in character, so there's a style about them that we mostly now only read about, and a nostalgia for a different era in the American dream.

Well, the closest I could come to it was the **Ridpath Hotel**, A very pleasant, mid-priced place where you can walk in off the street, or better still, feel that connection with the street that is lost with the car at a motel. But there's no nostalgia to it. The Ridpath has the restaurant and nightspot **Ankeney's** on the roof and the kind of shops you associate with the big hotels of the past, so if you're just hanging out for a convention, you can imagine yourself at the Ritz.

Sometime, on a trip to Spokane, I want to arrive by air, take a cab from the airport into town, and pull up to the **Spokane Sheraton**, for the weekend. It's a place built for pulling up to in cabs, a place where, if you feel like it and can afford it, you can hang out among the restaurants and lounges and be occupied and entertained, with the Convention Center and Opera House and Riverfront Park right nearby, for as long as you care to stay, with gentle forays to the shops and hubbub of downtown Spokane.

For seeing a city, to me it is essential to have a central base of operations. Except for the two hostelries mentioned so far, almost all the other accommodations are peripheral to the city center and cater to the automobile. The closest in are the two rather expensive **Cavanaugh's** on the north side of the river and a string of motels just off the freeway.

Since Spokane is a city of automobiles anyway, you might try driving out the old Sunset Highway and staying for the night at the **Spokane House**. Get onto Second Avenue heading west; as you leave the downtown center you begin to see Spokane on a smaller scale, from an earlier time. Spokane House commands a spectacular view of Spokane and the mountains to the east: specify a room high up on the east side. This place combines some of the qualities of a roadhouse from the fifties with an overlay of a slick chain motel operation. Its value is the view, and its proximity to many area sights. From here you can walk into the **Finch Arboretum**, or drive down into the canyon of the Spokane River for several scenic tours.

The Bed & Breakfast phenomenon has established itself in Spokane. On of the pleasures of staying in a b and b is that you often find yourself located in a neighborhood you might not otherwise see from the motel strip or downtown. For example, **Fotherington House** places you right in the heart of Browne's Addition west of town, in a district of elegant old houses, near museums, parks, and the Clarke Mansion, now **Patsy Clarke's**. Other b & b's are not so close in. To find current b & b listings, call **Spokane Bed & Breakfast**.

There are RV parks around the edges of Spokane: one, with proximity to the racetrack and the Fairgrounds, is **Park Lane**. For camping, **Riverside State Park**, provides a wonderful home base for a few days of forays around Spokane.

A QUICK LOOK

First, I must recommend the scenic drive. If you're short of time, and the weather's right (not, for example, in snow), you can whisk around Spokane following a series of directional arrowheads. As soon as you spot one, follow the sequence and keep your eyes peeled. You probably could hire a limosine to drive you around the route by calling **Spokane Carriage & Limousine Ltd**. Doing the whole route by bus is a bit tricky and requires several changes, perhaps better done over more than a day. Routes 45 and 7 to South Hill, 30 to Browne's Addition and 1, 2 and 5 to the north give you the most scenes, or call **Spokane Transit** for help planning routes. I especially like that part of the drive that takes you up onto the hills south of town, south of the freeway. It's an area you might not get to if you don't take the drive, but you shouldn't miss the streets of stately homes, Manito Park, clinging to the hills edge, and the remarkable **Cathedral of St. John the Evangelist**. You'll want to return to this part of town for the parks, maybe some walking tours, and to check out some of the odd places to visit. For, instance, you can get espresso up here, at **Lindaman's Gourmet to Go**.

A way to see the sights around downtown Spokane without the hassle of driving is to take the **Tour Train** from the old **Flour Mill**. It runs only in the months of good weather, and its hours might be a little erratic, so call for the current schedule. And of course you'll want to take the **Gondola Ride** swooping out over Spokane Falls from the west end of Riverfront Park.

Finally, for a quick overview of the city, **Gray Line Tours** does Spokane on a 2 1/2 hour sightseeing tour that leaves from the Greyound Depot every afternoon between May and October. Other, longer tours are scheduled to points of interest around the region.

A walking tour of Spokane can be intricate, and it can wear you out, as you are tempted to range farther afield in pursuit of the many unusual things to see. Here is a tour for the fairly hardy, which will give you a walking introduction to Spokane, one you can cut short at any point if you run out of steam.

Start out in the vicinity of Riverfront Park. There are plenty of places to put your car, if you have one, and no matter how short your walk, you will have seen some of the best of Spokane: the rehabilitation of the river and its recognition as the heart of the beauty and vitality of the city. You may want to save exploration of the park itself, site of the 1974 World Fair and spearhead of downtown renewal, for a later visit. But if your walk is a short one, wandering through the park gives you views of the center of town, many spots to stop and overlook the river and the falls, and a look at many of the old buildings illustrating the history of the town. I especially like the view of the downtown business district as seen from many vantage points around Riverfront Park. The architecture of the place is fascinating; some of it is bizarre; the juxtapositions of old, new and whacky make for happy surprises as the views unfold.

Crossing back and forth on the bridges over the river allows you to see several structures you may want to return to later, including the old flour mill on the north bank, now a complex of shops, and the Spokane County Courthouse. Its unlikely-looking fairy-tale structure you can get a good distant view of from the Monroe Street Bridge looking north. If you explore thoroughly you will have seen Spokane Falls with its power plant and remnant of the pumping station that didn't work during the big fire of '89. Also there is the spectacular gondola ride out over the falls, City Hall and across the street at the corner of the park that enthusiastic sculptural homage to the annual Bloomsday Marathon. And much else, too.

This peregrination should ultimately find you at the complicated intersection of Monroe Street and Riverside Avenue, where by turning in a slow circle you will see what I mean about Spokane's eclectic architecture: the deep red Spokesman-Review Building, in a Renaissance style similar to the courthouse; the Spokane Club, designed by Spokane's prolific turn-of-the-century architect Kirtland Cutter; the classic lines of the Masonic Temple; the Romanesque spires of Our Lady of Lourdes Cathedral.

Walking west (downriver) along Riverside Avenue, you enter a historic residential area called Browne's Addition. Luxurious homes and mansions built mostly in the 1880s and 90s recall the fortunes that came out of the mines of Idaho and Montana. If you walk west on Pacific to Poplar, then return on First or Second Avenue, checking out the cross streets as you go, you can view literally hundreds of homes ranging from the relatively modest frame structures of the period to Kirtland

Cutter's sumptuous extravagances. One of Cutter's finest efforts was the Patsy Clark Mansion built in 1897, now an elegant restaurant. While you're in the district you can round out your walk by visiting the **Cheney Cowles and Campbell Memorial Museums** where a house of Cutter's design is preserved.

To return, walk east along Sprague for a good look at the Davenport Hotel, then turn north on Howard, passing the **First National Bank** where you can see a fine series of murals commemorating the great fire, then the Bennett Block (of which more later) and arriving near your starting point, where you'll find a great cup of coffee at **Au Croissant**.

EATING OUT

I ran into a little trouble here. The number of restaurants in Spokane is staggering, even for a dedicated eater like myself. They range from fine dining in places with terrific views in mansions, hotels and motels, through the good solid eateries serving seafood, steaks and other specialties, to a myriad of fast food joints. The couple dozen that follow should get you started; notice that some additional good places are mentioned elsewhere, for example, **Ankeny's** in the nightlife section and the dining room at **Spokane House** under accomodations.

I hesitate to start out with **Patsy Clark's**, not wanting to give the impression I think it's the best restaurant in town. But it definitely is the fanciest, if also the most expensive. Because of its role in the history and visual attraction of the town, if you don't eat there you may wish you had. Architect Kirtland Cutter's most lavish private project among many, the mansion was for a while a museum. As a restaurant it retains much of that air--diners are expected to want to tour the place as part of their meal, and for a splendid night on the town, especially on a summer evening when you can stroll along the quiet streets of Browne's Addition, it's hard to beat in Spokane (I mean, they serve *escargot* there). If you just want to look at the place, you could stop in for a drink, or dessert.

For dinner with a view, and a mighty good steak, **Clinkerdagger's** in the Old Flour Mill, hanging right on the edge of Spokane Falls, has a spectacular vista right into the heart of downtown. Of the many steakhouses in the city, this is considered one of the best.

Next come the restaurants that give you a taste of Spokane as well as a good meal. One that comes immediately to mind is **Cyrus O'Leary's**, apparently one of the most popular eateries in town, located in an ornate section of the Bennett Block. Crowded with both locals and visitors, noisy with loud conversations and even louder music, and delightfully overdecorated, the place has a vast menu (lots of burgers) and the kind of chaos kids, especially teen-agers, like. Upstairs, at the opposite corner of this old building, you can find the opposite extreme in lunch and dinner atmosphere at **Moreland's**, a serious restaurant concentrating on fine cuisine, mostly French, albeit in a casual setting. On my visits it's been very quiet and mellow, the food excellent.

You may not expect to find terrific seafood in an inland city, but actually some restaurants here in Spokane seem to take more care with food from the sea than many restaurants on the water. **Milford's** is an old-time seafood spot that seems reminiscent of the early days of the city, with specials changing daily according to what's available fresh. If your cravings run to a late-night crustacean snack, you can have your pick of a wide variety of appetizers until one in the morning at the Seafood Bar at **C.I. Shenanegan's** overlooking the river-- of course there's standard dinner fare as well as seafood entrees in the restaurant.

Another seafood place, dressier but with the same insistence on fish fresh from the plane, is the **Regis Seafood Cafe**, a part of the elegant old St. Regis Hotel from years gone by. It has retained the marvelous decoration of a former era.

In almost every city you can find an inexpensive, hip, burgers and beer joint, not exactly a fern bar, but with some of the same quality of a gathering place for friends. In Spokane it looks like **The Onion Bar & Grill**, where they serve 28 different burgers, where you don't mind eating alone in the convivial atmosphere, where you might even meet somebody. The ornate antique bar, once a part of the old St. Regis Hotel, by itself is worth a visit.

International cuisine is well represented in Spokane, sometimes in rather uncommon ways. A discovery for me was **The Mustard Seed** across from the Opera House. It serves "nouveau oriental" cooking, a mixture of Japanese and Chinese with a dash of the Northwest style, in a very contemporary layout. Keep this place in mind for its after-theatre dinners. Nearby, at the **Suki Yaki Inn**, sushi, sashimi and other Japanese specialties are served in the traditional private tatami rooms. Always on the lookout for good Mexican food, I was heartened to find **Mission San Juan**. You'll want to return to this building on Wall for the other shops, mentioned elsewhere, and for this cantina-like restaurant, where they really seem to understand the concepts behind Mexican cooking. I like the ambience of those rambling family Italian places: one that's right downtown near the Ridpath is **Albertini's**. Finally, for Greek and Middle Eastern cooking, **Niko's** is in the heart of town and serves from a varied menu, with daily specials.

If you're a pizza fan, or traveling with kids, you'll want to know about **City Heights**. Close to Riverfront Park, with a big selection of imported beer, it has my vote as the Spokane pizza joint a parent could love. For pizza done in a different, and somewhat unusual style, seek out the Yugoslavian version at **Europa Pizza** in the Wall Street complex. And barbeque is made famous in Spokane by the **Longhorn Barbeque**, with its main dining location out toward the airport and several walk-up spots around town, including Riverfront Park.

Breakfasts can present a problem, if you want to find something outside the hotel or motel. If you like American breakfasts, try **Knight's Diner**, a nicely restored railroad car turned into a classic diner complete with a crackerjack at the grill and waitresses of great dexterity. It's sometimes crowded, but worth the wait. If you prefer the Continental style, **Au Croissant** operates its own bakery, so the croissants are *fresh* and the coffee, as I have said, is great.

A couple of places for treats: the neon and art deco **Ritzy's** for ice cream and other goodies; and **Early Dawn's Ice Creamery** for, um, the obvious. And to round out this list, a coffee house in the style of a coffee house, **Espresso Delizioso**, laid back, with books and journals at hand to read, and costumed patrons involved in their conversations; just like the old days.

PARKS

Parks are the traveler's great boon-- free, open, public spaces where one can escape the pressures of business or sightseeing. Looked at as a group, they seem to represent something about the town they are in, and a city's attitudes towards its parks reflect its attitudes toward urban amenities generally. Spokane has dedicated over 3,000 acres to public parks, ranging in style from the formal to the relatively wild and in use from intense to almost undisturbed. Its parks are a primary reason Spokane is such a pleasant place to be. As the very heart of town is a park, you get some idea of how the people here have chosen to live.

You've already been introduced to **Riverfront Park**, but it repays another visit. In building the World's Fair in 1974, acres of railroad yards, as well as two railway stations, were removed to make way for the fairgrounds. The visual impact was remarkable, judging from old photos I have seen, and it's easy to see, more than a decade later, the salutory effect such a massive renovation of the river's edge has had upon Spokane. All that remains of the railroading days is the clock tower from the Great Northern station, monument to a bygone era that in many ways is not missed. Other remnants, from the Fair itself, have been preserved and turned into activity centers and focus for the park. The central Pavilion has an ice arena in winter, an activity center for kids, and a couple of fast food spots. In summer months, the antique (1909) carousel delights kids and provides older folks with fond memories. The amphitheatre on the east side is still often used for outdoor concerts. Summertime brings even more energy with the **Public Market** and the **Arts & Crafts Marketplace** that fill up the days between Wednesday through Sunday from May through October. Just seeing the number of people on the rolling lawns on a gloriously hot summer day gives you an idea what a positive addition this park has been to the city.

Built around the turn of the century by famed landscape architect Frederick Ohlmstead (designer of New York's Central Park and Volunteer Park in Seattle), **Manito Park** is a crown of lilacs on the lilac city. This 90-acre landscape on South Hill has all the amenities of a traditional formal park: rose and lilac gardens; a Japanese garden; a greenhouse and collections of perennials; pools and formal paths. The best time to see these gardens is in late spring, when the roses and lilacs are blooming, but the park itself is a pleasure any time of year (the Japanese garden blanketed in snow; folks quietly ice-skating on the ponds). A gourmet picnic from the nearby **Lindaman's** on a spring day in Manito Park can make a lunch hour seem like another world.

The stately grace of the lawns and trees in the **Finch Memorial Arboretum** is unfortunately somewhat disturbed by the noise from major highways on either side of its long narrow prospect. But soon the noise fades from the mind as the eye is captured by ever more intriguing tree species, beautiful specimens of much-loved trees, fascinating grouping of varieties, and relationships of color and shape that keep the visitor wandering farther and farther along the paths. As with any well-made park, it needs to be visited through the seasons, to see the changing colors, shapes and emphases. One interesting note: you can walk down into the Arboretum from the Spokane House, another visual benefit of staying at that motel.

Two major parks on the west side of town to keep in mind are **High Bridge Park** along Latah Creek under the fragile-looking rail and road bridges that span the creek; and **Indian Canyon Park**, with its renowned golf course. In this park, along Rimrock Drive, there are places for picnics with sweeping panoramas of the river and the city.

Smaller parks dot the city. Two of particular interest to the visitor are **Coeur d'Alene Park** in Browne's Addition, where you can pause to rest or picnic during your arduous walking tour of old Spokane; and **Pioneer Park** right at the edge of South Hill overlooking the city, where you will find the **Corbin Art Center**.

To round out your parks visits I break a rule and include one that's out of town: **Riverside State Park** is about three miles downriver from Spokane, and if you're ready for a drive or a good long walk, you can see some marvelous terrain along this undeveloped stretch of the Spokane River. If you want to travel farther, you can have a look at the Little Spokane, which one source I read claims is the only wild river remaining in the state.

MUSEUMS

Mention has already been made of the **Cheney Cowles Memorial Museum**, in the heart of Browne's Addition, housed in a complex of former mansions and outbuildings typical of the architecture and splendidness of the area. The Cheney Cowles, operated by the Eastern Washington State Historical Society, is the city's major historical museum. As such, it contains the best collections from early Spokane and the development of the region. I found especially useful the extensive photo collection illustrating the architecture of Spokane, and enjoyed examining the diorama of Spokane Falls from about the time of the Great Fire. Other exhibits, especially of native artifacts, are fine, and the natural history section in the former coach-house is an excellent introduction to the flora and fauna of the area. Next door, the Grace Campbell home offers a chance to look closely at a Kirtland Cutter building, furnished and maintained in its turn-of-the-century style.

In a unique circular structure overlooking the river is housed the **Museum of Native American Culture**, considered one of the finest collections of Indian artifacts in the country. The collection of arrowheads and other stone points alone, despite their rather fanciful arrangements, is worth an afternoon's visit. And that's only one of 21 display galleries on the museum's five floors. Other collections include fine examples of Indian clothing, basketry and other implements. White culture is overly represented, it seems to me, for a native museum, but the contrasts and context those elements provide make one very much aware of the effects of the meeting of the two peoples. The quality of the displays is generally excellent, there is a fine collection of Western art, and outside, a pensive grove of tall slender totem poles stands guardian over the river.

If you're amused by contrasts, nearby on the Gonzaga University campus you can visit the **Bing Crosby Library** and view a collection of Crosby memorabilia, including gold records, Oscars, trophies, etc.

GALLERIES

There is a surprising number of art galleries in Spokane. The following is merely a selection; many of the galleries are chosen because they tie in with other points of interest you might be seeing. To find out more about current exhibits around town, the Friday Spokesman-Review "Weekend" section has a good gallery listing; or call the **Artsline** for more detailed information.

The **Cheney Cowles Museum** has an excellent permanent collection of regional art in all media, as well a space featuring current local and traveling shows. The **Spokane Public Library**, too, has a lively program of exhibits by local and regional artists. Another public exhibit space is the **Civic Theatre Gallery**, a community-supported theatre for use by local dramatic groups, that also presents area talent in the visual arts. And nearby the gallery at the **Spokane Art School** presents works by students and faculty, as well as occasional exhibits by invitation.

It's unusual, but very convenient, to find such a concentration of art exhibits as you'll see at S. 123 Madison. Three galleries share this address, sometimes in close cooperation, but more often in friendly co-existence. **Plexus Gallery**, **123 Arts**, and the **Lloyd Gallery** all show contemporary paintings, photography and work in other media from the region and around the country.

Intrigued by the name, I went once to **100% Realart** and was pleasantly surprised to find the 1985 National Works on Paper Exhibition, a field I'm especially interested in. It was traveling through, just as I was. It's that kind of serendipity that makes gallery hopping endlessly interesting.

A couple of other art galleries connected with educational institutions that you might like to look at while you're on the scenic tour are **Corbin Art Center Gallery** in Pioneer Park; and the **Spokane Falls Community College Gallery** near historic Fort Wright. Both these galleries show work primarily by students and instructors.

SHOPPING

Spokane's downtown merchants devised an ingenious system to beat the annual onslaught of snow and cold weather around here, and to emphasize the sense that shopping, especially in department stores and the like, is something you go around and *do* . The result is **The Skywalk**, enclosed walkways spanning the streets that link the major department stores, several shopping complexes including the handsome Bennet Block building and the massive Riverpark Square, as well as the two biggest parking garages in downtown Spokane. Even City Hall is connected. In effect what has been created is a downtown mall, something to combat the rush to the suburbs, and whatever you may think of the effect of cramming cars into the urban core, in Spokane at least it seems to be working.

Actually shopping along the Skywalk system is kind of a tour in itself, particularly in the Bennett Block and Riverpark Square, where the number of small shops should provide hours of poking around looking for the perfect souvenir. Along the way there are provisioners to keep you going: an Orange Julius place, **The Great American Cookie Co.**, and even a Chinese lunch, **The Dim**

Sum Inn. And Riverfront Park is never far away, so you can drop down to the street and go out and kick snow.

A similar concept, in a completely different style, has been put together at the old **Flour Mill**, a huge brick building across the river, which you can get to by walking through Riverfront Park. Twenty-six shops, including places for lunch, dinner and snacks, share space with nicely restored industrial remnants. You can get off your pins at an old-fashioned ice cream parlor, the **Sweet Treat Shoppe**, or browse the regional section at **The Book & Game Co**. You can continue your gallery hopping here, too, at **The Pottery Place**, claiming the largest selection of regional potters' work in the city; and **The Madkat Gallery** for posters and limited-edition prints.

Bookstores give the visitor ready access to a place-- local publications, books about the region and books by local authors augment the view from the streets, and bookstores often have the best bulletin boards for announcements of cultural events and other entertainments. In Spokane, the bookstore with the most charm and best selection is **Auntie's Bookstore & Cafe** at 313 Riverside. **B Dalton Bookseller** also has an excellent regional section . For the history of Spokane and environs, **Clarke's Old Book Store** deals in used and rare books and specializes in western Americana. And to return to the Atrium at 123 Wall, **Sun Tree Books** sells mostly metaphysical and well being books, but more important, has an excellent, up-to-date bulletin board outside its door. **Bookworld**, in Riverpark Square on the Skyway system, is a general-interest shop in an ideal place to cool out after traipsing all those tunnels.

If you haven't yet heard about Washington wines, here's your chance for an introduction. Spokane boasts of three wineries within its immediate vicinity, so you can take a short tour of the "wine country." For wine tasting in a spectacular setting, **Arbor Crest Winery** is located in a historic mansion high above the Spokane River. Some of the wines produced by **Latah Creek Winery** are so limited that they may be purchased only at the winery, so a visit there for tasting could be something special. At **Worden's Washington Winery** one of the top Reisling's in the state is produced, along with several other notable varietals.

A NIGHT ON THE TOWN

Whether you follow the symphony, hunt out the loudest rock 'n' roll you can find, or just want a little easy listening with dinner and maybe some dancing after, Spokane is able to meet any taste, almost any evening, or any time of year. Times I was there the place seemed to be jumping-- of course once was during the drag race championship. But I've also been there when the ballet season opened; not too shabby, either. Big events are held at the **Coliseum** and at the **Opera House**, and exhibitions and trade shows at the **Convention Center** next door. The reader board out front will give you a rough idea what's going on.

In an era when many community orchestras are in trouble, the **Spokane Symphony** seems healthy. Playing in the Opera House during a season September through April, the symphony balances its serious program with a strong showing in pops, and brings in a number of guest soloists and conductors. Dance, too, has its devoted followers. The **Spokane Ballet**, one of the Northwest's most prestigious companies, plays the Opera House.

The group **Spokane Musical Arts** puts on a wide variety of events during the concert season. Performances range from chamber ensembles to jazz sessions, and take place at a number of different halls around town. Another series is called **Connoisseur Concerts** and presents chamber music also at the city's various auditoriums. Also check the bulletin boards at the major churches, where many of the serious music events are held. Incidentally, the organs at both the Cathedral of St. John the Evangelist and St. Aloysius on the Gonzaga campus are superb.

Resident theatre groups seem to be holding their own, too. **Spokane Civic Theatre** has been well-supported by the community over the years. It plays in a versatile building which also houses the more intimate Studio Theatre and an art gallery.

In a nicely restored and maintained older theatre right downtown, the **Interplayers Ensemble** packs a lot of activity into a season that includes visiting performers as well as plays presented by the resident troupe. Children's theatre comes in the form of the **Magic Lantern Theatre** working out of the Atrium on Wall.

To get on with the music: Jazz clubs have come and gone in Spokane; they are fragile enough things even in much larger cities, and I'm afraid I can't come up with one right now. However, the **Spokane Jazz Society** puts on periodic big events and if you call somebody there might have other ideas. The local ensemble Jazz Conspiracy plays steady gigs around town including Ankeny's and weekend jams at the **Gung Ho**.

There's a real gamut of nightclubs. You take the elevator up to the top of the Ridpath, and step out into this polished black, shiny chrome, with plants and big plate windows restaurant and lounge **Ankeny's**, where there's entertainment nightly, as they say, the dining is top rate, and the view terrific. Not bad, and you can get pretty much the same deal at any of the major hotels and motels, so it depends a lot on where you're staying-- or, if you want to *feel* like you're staying in a place like a Cavanaugh's, you can go to dinner there, or take in a show, rub elbows and drive on back out to the campground after. In-room guides, the newspaper (especially Friday's), and usually some kind of reader-board will let you know who's playing what as you look around town.

For the other clubs, you start with what you want to hear. **Ahab's Whale** has been presenting rock 'n' roll for years. Other rock emporiums include **Fun City** and **Henry's Pub**. You get some rock 'n' roll in the cantina at the **Casa Blanca**, but the program is varied there, so you might want to check.

For country/western sounds there's **The Stockyards**, a mighty steakhouse, dancehall and good-time spot. Or drop in for a brew at **Tilly's Tavern**, and catch some of the country sounds there.

And if you're in town to play the ponies you might like to hang out at **The Flame** right next to the Playfair Racetrack, where the racetrack crowd goes, so they say, and where there's also a card room, if there's anything left after the races.

INDOOR & OUTDOOR SPORTS

Because of the famous racetracks, both cars and

horses, Spokane is an exciting place for spectator sports. The thoroughbred racing track, **Playfair**, has a season from the end of April till the end of October, has a huge and popular restaurant, and all the slick accoutrements of the sport. Playfair is close enough to the downtown center that it's easy to make a balmy summer evening at the races part of your visit. One thing I didn't know about Spokane (till I showed up during one) is that it hosts the American Hot Rod Association drag racing championships every year, a huge event that draws well over a hundred thousand spectators and several hundred entries to **Spokane Raceway Park**. Drag race season runs through the hot, noisy days of summer, but if you love fast cars .... Raceway Park also has a stockcar track and other racing facilities.

Participating in sports is also easy in Spokane. In fact, there are so many public golf courses, swimming pools and the like, that I've concentrated here on some of the sports that might make a visit more an expression of the place. The first thing that came to my mind was white water rafting, on that stretch of river below Spokane Falls. Some say it's dangerous, so if you're just checking it out, get in touch with somebody who knows the water, like **River Odysseys West** or **North Star Wilderness Co**. Apparently the rafting depends to some extent on the time of year, too, so advance information seems advisable. River rafting above the falls is slow and leisurely.

For a look at a different Spokane, try a horseback ride through the rough terrain and scant pines of Indian Canyon Park. **Last Chance Riding Stables** rents horses, gauged to your ability. It's a way to imagine the place without the houses and highways.

Winter sports are of course a tremendous attraction, even though most of the skiing goes on in the surrounding regions (Mt. Spokane, for instance, is considered one of the prime ski areas in the state). For tips and gossip and ski gear, **Lou-Lou's** is an outfitter you should know about. Some of the city's golf courses, like **Indian Canyon**, allow crosscountry skiing during the winter, and a little searching will turn up other ways to play in the snow. I mentioned the winter ice rink at Riverfront Park; there is ice skating on ponds in some of the parks, for instance the big pond in Manito Park. Indoor rinks include the **Lilac City Ice-A-Rena**, and the Coliseum, where the ice hockey games are held.

I should probably mention jogging and running as a way to see Spokane-- there's a good track at **Shadle Park**-- but in Spokane running, both for spectators and participants, ranks as a Big Event.

BIG EVENTS

In early May, when the snow is gone, the falls exuberantly roaring and the city's flowers at full bloom, Spokane holds its annual celebration, **The Lilac Festival.** It runs for about ten days and involves nearly every segment of the community. And one of the biggest crowds of the year assembles during these festivities for the annual **Bloomsday Run**. Runners and spectators literally fill the streets for this fun run that winds through several miles of city streets. Lilac Festival time is a great time to visit Spokane.

Big events pop up the calendar round. I mentioned the drag race finals, in August. The **Spokane Interstate Fair** in September is followed by autumn events like the symphony and ballet openings. Winter brings the **Inland Empire Arts & Crafts Show** and **Ag Expo** among others, and in early spring the **Diamond Spur Rodeo** to the Coliseum. For the year's event calendar, or a monthly guide, call the **Convention and Visitors Bureau** and get on a mailing list.

Well that's Spokane. It grows on you. I could have done a whole chapter on the parks, the architecture and the history. It's a place I wouldn't mind staying awhile.

Spokane Club 1910.

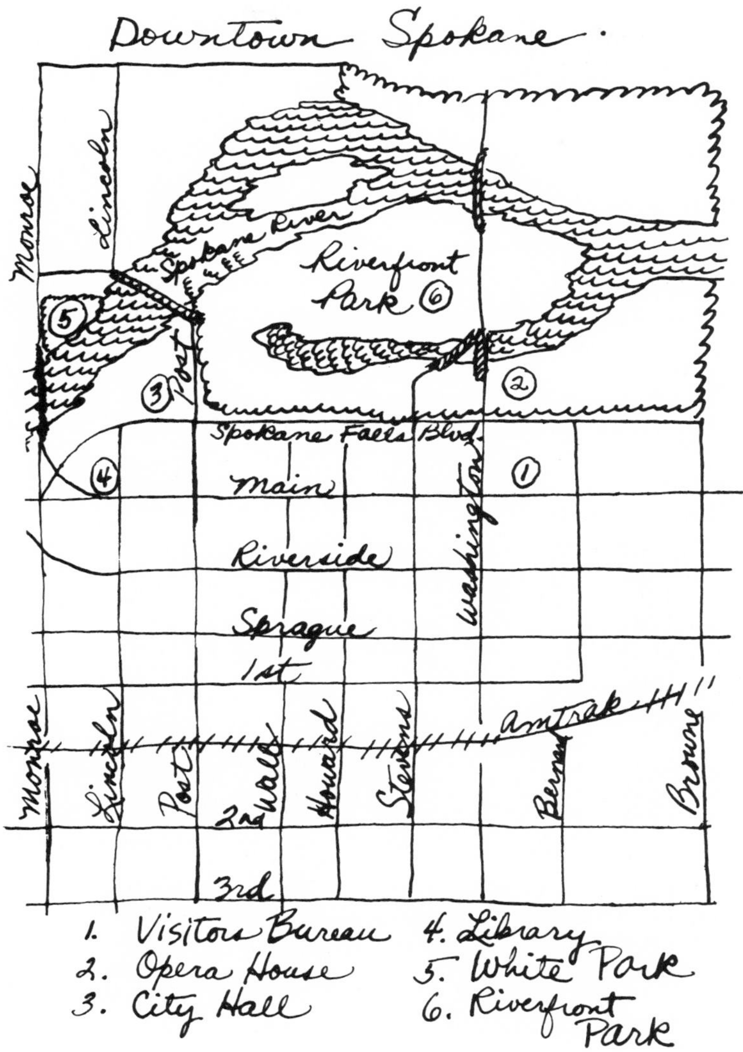

1. Visitors Bureau
2. Opera House
3. City Hall
4. Library
5. White Park
6. Riverfront Park

Spokane Index

747-0317

EARLY DAWN'S ICE CREAMERY....................239
Parkade Plaza
624-9923

ESPRESSO DELIZIOSO....................239
S. 123 Wall
455-6788

EUROPA PIZZA....................239
S. 125 Wall
455-4051

FINCH ARBORETUM.......232
W. 3404 Woodland Blvd.
747-2894

FIRST NATIONAL BANK....................236
W. 502 Riverside
455-6400

FLAME....................249
E. 2401 Sprague
535-5500

FLOUR MILL..............233, 246
W. 621 Mallon

FORT WRIGHT
W. 4000 Randolph Rd.

FOTHERINGHAM HOUSE VICTORIAN BED AND BREAKFAST....................232
2128 W. Second Ave.
838-4363

FRIENDS OF THE DAVENPORT....................231
Info: 838-8785

FUN CITY....................249
N. 808 Division
325-9220

GONDOLA RIDES............234
S.W. Corner Riverfront Park
747-1437

GONZAGA UNIVERSITY
E. 502 Boone
328-4220

GRAYLINE TOURS............234
W. 910 Sprague
455-5055

GREAT AMERICAN COOKIE COMPANY.......245
W. 814 Main
747-0414

GREYHOUND BUS DEPOT....................228
W. 1125 Sprague
624-5251

GUNG HO RESTAURANT....................249
N. 1303 Division
328-5321

HENRY'S PUB....................249
W. 230 Riverside
624-9828

RIDPATH HOTEL...............231
515 Sprague
838-2711

RITZY'S 239
W. 702 Third
747-8800

RIVERFRONT PARK.........240
Spokane Falls Blvd.
456-5512

RIVER ODYSSEYS
WEST..250
534-2024

RIVERSIDE STATE
PARK.......................................233
456-2499

SHADLE PARK AND
POOL.......................................251
Longfellow and Ash
456-2620

SHERATON
SPOKANE.............................331
N. 322 Spokane Falls Court
455-9600

SPOKANE ART
SCHOOL...............................244
N. 902 Howard
328-0900

SPOKANE BALLET............248
W. 820 Sprague
747-0360

SPOKANE BED AND
BREAKFAST
RESERVATION
SERVICE.................................232
Info: 624-3770

SPOKANE CARRIAGE AND
LIMOUSINE, LTD.............233
S. 621 Freya
534-5515

SPOKANE CIVIC
THEATRE...............................248
N. 1020 Howard
325-1413

SPOKANE CONVENTION
CENTER.................................247
W. 334 Spokane Falls Blvd.
456-6006

SPOKANE FALLS
COMMUNITY
COLLEGE GALLERY..........245
W. 3410 Fort Wright Dr.
459-3710

SPOKANE HOUSE............232
(Quality Inn)
W. 4301 Sunset Hy.
838-1471

SPOKANE
INTERNATIONAL
AIRPORT..............................229
I-90 West of City
624-3218

Afterword:

If you have information about spots to explore, things to do or places to stay in your "smaller city", let us hear from you. Or, if your town plans annual celebrations and special events we might have missed here, let us know.

WRITE: **SMALLER CITIES**
c/o Quartzite Books
P. O. Box 1931
Mount Vernon, WA 98273

Road marker
Pullman.